OTHER BOOKS BY JESWALD W. SALACUSE

Making Global Deals: Negotiating in the International Marketplace

International Business Planning: Law and Taxation (with William P. Streng, six volumes)

Social Legislation in the Contemporary Middle East (co-editor with Laurence Michalak)

An Introduction to Law in French-Speaking Africa: North Africa

An Introduction to Law in French-Speaking Africa: Africa South of the Sahara

Nigeria Family Law (with A. B. Kasunmu)

THE ART OF ADVICE

THE ART
OF ADVICE

HOW TO GIVE IT
AND HOW TO TAKE IT

JESWALD W. SALACUSE

TIMES ⒯ BOOKS

RANDOM HOUSE

Library of Congress Cataloging-in-Publication Data

Salacuse, Jeswald W.
    The art of advice : how to give it and how to
take it / Jeswald W. Salacuse. — 1st ed.
        p.   cm.
    Includes bibliographical references.
    ISBN 0-8129-2102-X
    1. Consultants.   2. Counseling.   3. Helping
behavior.   I. Title.   II. Title: Advice.
BF637.C56S255   1994
158'.3—dc20   93-44596

Manufactured in the United States of America
98765432

First Edition

Book design by Warren Infield

For Bill and Maria, both advisors and clients

CONTENTS

PREFACE

This book has arisen out of my thirty years of experience in educating a wide variety of professionals, from judges and lawyers to business executives and diplomats, from governmental administrators and economic policy planners to corporate counsel and independent consultants. That experience, both in the United States and abroad, constantly revealed that advising and counseling are key functions in every profession but that professionals are rarely, if ever, specifically trained in those important skills. Time and time again, whether dealing with professionals in a corporate boardroom in New York or a government office in Cairo, I saw that the ability to be an effective advisor was often the difference between success and failure on the job, and that failure as an advisor was usually not due to a lack of substantive knowledge about a specific technical subject, but rather to an absence of understanding about the process of actually giving useful advice.

My goal in this book is to provide basic guidance on how to give advice effectively. It is aimed at all professionals—indeed, all persons who seek to help others through advice. Advising is a basic form of human interaction. Principles exist that can make that interaction fruitful for both advisors and clients. The purpose of this book is to identify those principles and to explain how they should be applied.

In writing *The Art of Advice*, I have drawn on a variety of sources. I have examined the specialized literature of various professions on advising and counseling, and have also relied on my own experience as consultant over the last three decades to governments, businesses, universities, individuals, nonprofit institutions, and international organizations in various parts of the world. I have also greatly benefited from lengthy interviews with experienced advisors in several professions. Their insights enriched my writing immeasurably. I therefore owe thanks to Peter Ackerman; Douglas Bailey; Keith Highet, Esq.; Harland A. Riker, Jr.; Richard Norton, M.D.; George Kidder; Elliot L. Richardson; William F. McSweeny; Rev. William McLennan (who also read and commented on a chapter of the manuscript); and Thomas Yeomans, Ph.D. I also want to thank the many other persons with whom I have had conversations over the years on the art of advising.

Donna Booth Salacuse, my wife, and Professor Jeffrey Z. Rubin, my colleague, read and meticulously commented upon the entire manuscript. I am grateful for their many insights. During the course of writing the book, I also received valuable help from student research assistants at the Fletcher School of Law and Diplomacy. They are Rima Hartzenbusch, Theodore

Johnson, and Tammy Halevy. I also owe thanks to Henry Ferris, my editor at Times Books, to Barney Karpfinger, my agent, and to Jean Callahan, my assistant at the Fletcher School, who meticulously prepared the manuscript while superbly carrying out her many other duties at that institution.

THE ART OF ADVICE

1

ADVISORS
AND
CLIENTS

**"He who relies entirely on his own
judgment ever regrets it."**
—Ibn Iskandar, A *Mirror for Princes*

THE WORLD RUNS ON ADVICE. From the White House to the
day care center, professional and personal advice drives count-
less decisions and actions every day in all areas of life. Few
governments, companies, organizations, or individuals take
significant actions without first seeking the help of a consultant, counselor, mentor, tutor, guide, or advisor. Everyone
gives and takes advice at one time or another. All of us are
both advisors and clients.

Giving advice is a basic task of all professions. Doctors,
lawyers, economists, engineers, financiers, and ministers
spend a large part of each working day recommending what
other people should do. While the lawyer's opinion letter, the
engineer's report, the physician's consultation, and the money
manager's recommendations draw on different bodies of
knowledge, each is advice to someone—advice that leads to
actions having far-reaching consequences.

Advice is also an essential management tool in corporations. Subordinates influence their bosses' decisions through advice, and most boardroom decisions are the product of advice from many sources, both inside and outside the company. Bosses, too, know that it is often better to advise employees on a particular course of action, rather than to give them direct orders. While "advice" from the boss is in some cases merely a disguised command, in many situations, particularly when authority has been broadly delegated in the organization, a manager plays a genuine advisory role. Generally speaking, the more decentralized the operation and the more educated the employees, the more important advice becomes in running a business.

The ability to make a sale or serve a customer often depends on the quality of advice that goes with a product or service. Thus computer salespersons, stockbrokers, building contractors, and mortgage bankers, each in their own way, must be effective, reliable advisors to succeed in today's competitive business environment. Too often, unfortunately, they neglect or even fail to acknowledge their role as advisor. For many hard-driving salespersons, their job is to sell, not advise.

In government, advisors have always played a crucial role in making and executing policy. Throughout history, counselors to kings and emperors have influenced decisions about peace and war. Machiavelli, Richelieu, and Rasputin shaped the course of events in Italy, France, and Russia, respectively, through their advice. In more recent times, Americans have become accustomed to seeing such unelected advisors as Clark Clifford, Henry Kissinger, Abe Fortas, and Robert Strauss wield power through their ability to counsel presidents.

Indeed, the advisor, both officially and unofficially, seems to be a permanent fixture of modern public administration. Throughout the country, national, state, and local governments rely on advisors for assistance on everything from military strategy to zoning regulations. Outside the United States, many nations, most recently in Eastern Europe and in what used to be the Soviet Union, actively seek *foreign* advisors to help them solve difficult economic and political problems with which they have had little experience, like creating market economies or constitutional governments.

Many advisors are committees. Indeed, the advisory committee seems to be a permanent feature of modern bureaucracies. The federal government, for example, has over a thousand officially constituted advisory committees—so many, in fact, that Congress had to pass a special law, the Federal Advisory Committee Act, to regulate them. The reason governments and corporations use committees instead of individuals as advisors is not only to obtain a broadened base of information but also to create a forum in which different viewpoints within the organization may be shaped into a single recommendation for action.

In addition to these traditional types of advisors, the modern era, with its emphasis on information, has witnessed the rise of new occupations whose fundamental purpose is to advise. Financial planners, nutrition consultants, personal fitness trainers, and crisis hot-line attendants, among others, exist to give advice. With the growth of the modern information society, other kinds of advisors will certainly come on the scene. Moreover, traditional professions such as medicine and law may find that their advisory roles will become even more important in the future. For example, if the medical profession is to emphasize disease prevention, as many experts urge, doctors will have to become more skilled in advising patients about ways to stay healthy.

In an information society, the advisor is crucial. The advisor processes and makes usable the vast amounts of information that society accumulates at an ever-accelerating pace. If information is indeed a basic commodity in today's world, advice is the finished product. The advising process adds value to raw information. We may indeed live in the information age, but we also live in the age of advice.

ADVISING IS AN ART

Giving advice is an art. Some people do it well. Others, often equally knowledgeable, do it poorly. The difference between the two is that the poor advisor is not skilled or trained in the art of advice. Like any art, giving advice is governed by certain basic principles—principles which apply to all professions. The ineffectual advisor has failed to learn and apply those principles. The skilled advisor, on the other hand, has mastered them to the point that their application is virtually automatic. The ability of a lawyer, engineer, minister, or physician to help another person with a problem will in many cases depend as much on a mastery of the art of advice as on a substantive knowledge of law, engineering, theology, or medicine.

Despite the important role of advice in modern life, professional schools and executive training programs devote little attention to teaching about the process of actually giving advice to the clients and customers their students one day will serve. (Indeed, they often give their students attitudes and ideas that actually impede effective advising.) Instead, schools and programs concentrate almost exclusively on teaching the substantive knowledge that is the basis of professional advice. Most lawyers leave law school without formal training in advising clients. Economists receive Ph.D.s without having read anything on exactly how they should go about giving advice to governments and corporations. Management consultants undertake million-dollar assignments without a thorough grounding in the process of actually counseling troubled companies. With rare exceptions, both academic journals and popular books are generally silent about the process of giving advice. The small amount of professional literature on the subject tends to take a narrow, parochial view. So legal counseling is seen as quite separate and distinct from medical advising, and both are viewed as having nothing whatsoever to do with management consulting. While many books and articles do discuss consulting, they are concerned primarily with how to organize and operate a consulting business. What they usually do not discuss is the consultant's basic challenge: how to give good advice.

Substantive knowledge of law, medicine, or engineering is certainly essential for a lawyer, doctor, or consulting engineer, but that knowledge alone is not sufficient. An effective advisor must understand both the *substance* and the *process* of giving advice. Advice is both product and process.

The Art of Advice is about the process of giving advice. It offers advice about advice. It is based on the notion that all advising is governed by certain common principles regardless of the profession or area of life in which the advisor works. The principles discussed apply in a doctor's clinic, a lawyer's office, a government agency, and even in your own kitchen when you try to counsel your less-than-cooperative teenager. By explaining the principles of the art of advice, this book seeks to improve the effectiveness of advisors in a wide range of professions, from doctors, lawyers, and engineers to media consultants, nutrition advisors, and hot-line attendants. It also hopes to make advice a more recognized management tool within the business world generally. This book is also about taking advice. By setting out the principles of the art of advice, it tries to give the users of advice a way to evaluate their advisors and the advice they give. The book, then, is concerned with both artistry and art appreciation.

THE MANY FORMS OF ADVICE

Advice, like art, comes in many forms—calls from your stockbroker when the market is falling, newspaper columns on coping with teenagers, suggestions from your boss on how to deal with a difficult customer, recommendations from your doctor on changing your diet, policy papers to the president on negotiating with the Japanese over trade barriers. Advice may be solicited and unsolicited. It may be addressed to a specific individual or to a general class of people. Despite differences in form, *all advice is essentially a communication from one person to another for the purpose of helping the second person determine a course of action for solving a particular problem.* An advisor's basic task is to help clients make decisions.

ORACLES AND ATTENDANTS

Precisely how an advisor helps a client determine a course of action depends on how the advisor sees his or her role. Advisors can play a whole spectrum of roles. At one extreme are advisors who view themselves as oracles, individuals who, after receiving an appropriate appeal from a supplicant, pronounce an opinion just like the oracle did in the temple of Delphi in ancient Greece. For the oracle advisor, the client is an empty vessel to be filled with the advisor's wisdom. Once the oracle has spoken, it is up to the client to follow the advice. Most of us have at one time or another encountered an oracle advisor. Traditionally, many doctors have tended to see themselves as the oracle when they advised their patients on health problems.

At the other end of the spectrum are advisors who consider themselves attendants of their clients. Like temple attendants of ancient times, attendant advisors exist to serve their clients. They believe that their basic task is to help the client draw on his or her own knowledge and experience in determining a course of action necessary to solve the client's problem. The attendant does not consider the client to be an empty vessel but rather an important, if not primary, source of information and knowledge. This type of advisor sees his or her role as helping the client identify, organize, evaluate, and apply knowledge and information that the client already has. Psychotherapists have traditionally seen themselves as attendant advisors.

Between the oracle advisor at one end of the spectrum and the attendant advisor at the other there is a wide range of advisor roles, characterized by two factors:

1. The extent to which the advisor draws on the client's knowledge, experience, and information.
2. The extent to which the client participates in determining the proposed course of action that he or she is to take.

The following diagram is illustrative:

RANGE OF ADVISORY ROLES

ORACLE   ATTENDANT

Increasing Client Input ⟶

Decreasing Advisor Domination ⟶

The oracle accepts little or no input from the client and pronounces the advice to be followed completely. The attendant advisor, on the other hand, obtains as much information as possible from the client and allows the client to determine the course of action to solve the problem. As one moves along the spectrum from oracle to attendant, the input of the client increases in the advising process as the domination of the advisor recedes.

THE NATURE OF ADVICE

Good advice, whether given by an oracle or offered by an attendant, is usually aimed at having the client take or refrain from taking a particular action. Sometimes people believe they are giving advice when in fact they are merely stating a fact or expressing an opinion, with no explicit recommendation on a course of action. For example, when your stockbroker calls to say that IBM earnings fell in the most recent quarter, she is stating a fact. If in addition to that fact, she says the price of IBM will decline, she is giving an opinion, but without suggesting what you should do. It is when she recommends that you sell your IBM stock that she is giving advice, for it is only then that she is suggesting a definite course of action. Whether an advisor's statement is actionable cannot be determined from the statement alone; it also depends on the knowledge that the client has and brings to the advising process. So it is important for any advisor to determine what the client knows about the subject under consideration.

Many people called "advisors" do not really advise at all. Some advisors—for example, researchers in congressional offices—may gather information or analyze data but stop short of recommending a definite course of action to their boss. They may be part of the advising process, but they themselves are not giving advice. Other advisors have the basic task of implementing decisions or policies, and they, too, are not actually engaged in giving advice. And in many companies that have laid off workers, independent "consultants" do the jobs formally done by hourly employees. These consultants are not really advisors.

Advising someone is a *process*—a progressive movement toward an end. That end is the determination of a course of action that will help a client solve a problem. The advisor organizes and manages the advising process—a process that involves many persons, especially the client.

An essential characteristic of advice is that the client is free to accept or reject it. Advice therefore differs from an order or command that the recipient is bound to follow. In practice, of course, clients may feel little freedom to reject authoritative advice. A cancer patient may see no choice but to accept radical surgery recommended by a specialist as the only feasible option to avoid a premature death. A poor country seeking a loan from the International Monetary Fund may have no alternative to accepting IMF advice to devalue its currency and cut budgetary subsidies. Nonetheless, the essence of advice is the legal or theoretical right of the client to reject it. Cancer patients and poor countries have that right, even though they may choose not to use it. An advisor who fails to respect the client's right of rejection sometimes loses that client.

It is important to distinguish the process of advising from the process of implementing advice. The precise boundary between the two processes is sometimes vague, since the same individual may both give advice and then be asked by the client to implement it. A surgeon recommends surgery to a patient and then performs the operation. A management consultant proposes new budgeting procedures to a company and then proceeds to install them. A legislative consultant recommends that a senator introduce a new law and then writes the bill. The focus of this book, however, is advice, not implementation.

ADVISING IS A RELATIONSHIP

Advising is essentially a relationship between two parties, the advisor and the client. It is a relationship based on trust— so much so that Sir Francis Bacon declared that "the greatest trust between man and man is the trust of giving counsel."*
It is a two-way relationship in which both advisor and client have to participate. How well they manage that relationship will determine the effectiveness of the advising process. Let's look briefly at the two parties:

The Advisor: An Expert, a Bridge, a Son of a Bitch from Out of Town

The reason one person is an advisor and another a client is that the advisor is supposed to know something useful that the

---

* "Of Counsel," *Essays.*

client does not. Specialized knowledge gives one the potential to become an advisor. But being an expert is not enough. Advisors must be able to relate their expertise to the world of the client. The advisor is therefore a bridge between the world of expertise and the world of the client. An estate lawyer is a bridge between the world of law and the world of family finance. The public relations consultant bridges the worlds of business and the world of the media. A former government official becomes a consultant in Washington precisely because he or she has the ability to forge links between the world of business and the world of the federal bureaucracy. Sometimes, however, consultants, particularly those with arcane specializations, do not recognize the importance of their bridging function until they have gained some experience. Sometimes they never do. The key to an advisor's real effectiveness does not lie in technical expertise, but rather in the ability to apply that expertise to the client's situation. Experts who are unable to bridge those two worlds usually fail as advisors.

Demand for new types of advisors arise when knowledge develops and people feel a need to apply that knowledge to their lives. In the 1960s, as the technologies of television, public polling, and computers advanced, politicians sensed a potential for their use in political campaigning but knew little about them. At that time the world of politics and the world of the new technologies were quite separate and distinct. If politics was to harness these new technologies, the two worlds would have to be bridged. So a group of professionals emerged to apply communications and computer technologies to election campaigns. They were political consultants, who today have become indispensable to any campaign. They have bridged the two worlds.

Sometimes an advisor's contribution is not new knowledge,

but a fresh perspective. The injection of a new perspective may slow down or stop reckless action and provide an opportunity for the client to have useful second thoughts about a course of action. For example, an executive who decides in anger to quit his job may be kept from making a bad mistake if he first seeks the advice of a senior colleague. On the other hand, the fresh perspective of an advisor may stimulate action by a person or company that had previously been bogged down with indecision.

The fact that an advisor has less responsibility and fewer links to a client organization than an employee has certain advantages. If a company's internal structure and dynamics inhibit creative thinking and new ideas by its employees, an outside consultant may be the only means to inject creativity into the organization. Ironically, the type of person the company would engage as a consultant in that case may be exactly the type it would never hire as an employee. Being an advisor also allows a person to be more objective and detached concerning such matters as quality of performance and the productivity of employees than if he or she were a full-time member of the organization. That very detachment may be the precise reason why the client chose an advisor in the first place.

Yet an advisor's detachment from the organization, when coupled with the power granted by the boss, may cause fear and anxiety among the company's employees. Often the appearance of an advisor on the scene is a sign that major changes are on the horizon—budgets will be cut, programs abolished, departments closed, executives dismissed. For the company's employees, a consultant is neither a wise expert nor a bridge to new technology; he is simply, to use an old navy expression, "a son of a bitch from out of town."

An advising relationship has both benefits and costs. It is

important for both the advisor and the client to understand those costs and benefits so as to manage that relationship in a way that is advantageous for both parties. Let us look at the benefits and costs to the advisor.

The Benefits of Being an Advisor

People become advisors for many reasons. Both advisor and client must understand that motivation for the sake of their relationship. Understanding advisors' motivations can help clients to evaluate the advice they receive. For those in an advising profession, a primary motivation is, of course, money. Millions of professionals throughout the United States—lawyers, doctors, financial analysts, business consultants—earn their living by giving advice to other people. But other reasons—prestige, power, friendship, idealism—may also lead a person to offer advice. Parents advise their children out of love and concern for their welfare. A senior manager may offer career counseling to a junior executive because of idealism, or because the act of advising gratifies his ego. An advisor need not receive a fee in order to derive benefits out of the relationship. Many advisors to political leaders have gained significantly from their position. If power is the ability to influence the course of events, then being an advisor to presidents is a form of power to the extent that the advisor influences presidential decisions.

Some people choose to become advisors as a way of avoiding relationships that may entail increased risks and responsibilities. For example, rather than become an employee of a company, a relationship that would prohibit working for other firms, a management expert may prefer to structure his or her relationship with that company as an advisor or consultant. One highly paid Washington lawyer and friend of presidents consistently refused to accept a cabinet post because it would have reduced his income significantly since he would have had to abandon his lucrative law practice. Instead, he served as an unpaid presidential advisor. A few years ago in Texas, as banks were failing and their directors faced lawsuits, a professor of finance resigned his directorship of a troubled bank and immediately became an advisor to the board of directors, a position that allowed him to attend board meetings and collect an "advisor's fee"—which, incidentally, was the same amount paid to directors for attending board meetings. While he felt greater security through this maneuver, it is not certain that a court would have agreed that he was in reality an advisor instead of a director.

And finally, a person may assume the role of advisor as a tactic to influence another for the advisor's benefit. The element of reliance that is implicit in the advisory relationship increases the advisor's power to influence the client. Thus a senior partner in a firm may become an advisor to a younger, valued associate in order to dissuade the associate from taking a job offer from a competing firm. Or an auto salesperson may try to become an advisor to an elderly customer in order to persuade the customer to buy a car.

Clients: Looking for Someone to Lean On

Clients, like advisors, come in many forms and have many names—"patient," "customer," "advisee," "account." Some actively seek advice; others need to be persuaded that they need it. In general, a client is a person who seeks the professional advice of another person in order to solve a problem. The word *client* comes from the Latin *cliens*—"a person who has someone to lean on." Inherent in the advisor-client relationship is the notion of trust and reliance by the client on the advisor. The specific degree of reliance will vary from relationship to relationship. The trust that a patient puts in a doctor is, of course, greater than the reliance of a fitness enthusiast on a trainer. But in all cases the advisor, by offering advice to another, is implicitly asking that person to rely on the advisor's knowledge and expertise.

The Benefits of Advice

Clients use advisors for many reasons. If an advisor is to perform effectively, he or she must understand precisely why the client is seeking help. The most common reason is that the advisor has expertise that the client needs: the client is deficient in some way, and the advisor has the knowledge or skill to make up for that deficiency. For example, political leaders use advisors because of such perceived deficiencies as lack of specialized knowledge, limited time to handle a heavy workload, or an overly partisan viewpoint.

But a perceived deficiency is not the only reason for a client to seek an advisor. A client may choose an advisor in order to influence people or organizations with whom the client has to deal. Eastern European governments, in reforming their economies, choose distinguished foreign economists as advisors not only to learn about market economies but also to encourage western governments and international organizations to provide aid. Candidates running for national office will choose particular political consultants as a means to persuade wealthy sponsors to finance their campaigns. In these cases, the choice of advisor is, in effect, a message to third parties of the client's policies and intentions.

Advisors are also chosen to justify an action that the client has already decided to take. A company chairman, determined to close down a subsidiary, may first commission a consultant's study of the subsidiary's performance and then announce the closing after receiving the consultant's report recommending the action. Governments that are not politically strong enough to implement economic austerity on their own will often justify those measures on the grounds that they have been recommended by the International Monetary Fund.

Some clients merely want ornamental advisors. A client may choose an advisor to share the advisor's prestige or fame. The shadowy Bank of Credit and Commerce International hired a prestigious Washington law firm primarily to increase the bank's legitimacy in government circles and improve its access to the federal bureaucracy. Even legitimate companies may engage famous consultants like Henry Kissinger in order to increase their own prestige by association.

And finally, a person may ask the advice of another as a tactic to influence the advisor. It is always flattering to be asked for advice. In effect, by asking for advice a client is paying tribute to the advisor's wisdom, knowledge, and insight. Such flattery, it is hoped, will make the advisor more amenable to influence by the client. Thus, job seekers often begin an interview with a possible employer by asking for advice on career guidance. And negotiators may try to soften up an adversary by asking for his or her advice on a proposed contract.

It is important for any advisor to understand why a client is seeking help. Advisors ought not to assume that their wisdom and knowledge are the only factors that influenced a client's decision to retain them.

THE COSTS OF ADVICE

Advice, even when it is free, has costs. In addition to understanding the benefits that the client is seeking, an advisor should also be aware of the costs that the client is paying for the relationship. The advisor's fee is only one of the costs. In addition, an advisor's counsel may turn out to be wrong and therefore cause the client to incur greater costs than he would have if he had followed another course of action. The skilled advisor also recognizes that there are other potential costs to the client and seeks to carry out the advising relationship in a way that will minimize them. Several non-monetary costs are potentially present in every advising relationship.

Loss of Control

A major cost for clients entering an advising relationship is the potential loss of control over their affairs, their businesses, or their lives. Once on the scene, the advisor has the potential to influence matters that were once the client's alone to control. Sick people resist becoming patients because they fear that their doctors, not they, will control their lives. Seeking a lawyer's help in a dispute with your neighbor may lead to a lawsuit that you never thought you would ever initiate. Skilled advisors recognize this fear in their clients and take steps to assure their clients that they, not their advisors, are in control of the problem and their lives.

Loss of Status

In seeking advice, a client acknowledges an inability to deal with a problem. For certain individuals, engaging an advisor therefore represents a loss of status or prestige, because they fear that other people will judge them as less competent or knowledgeable than was first assumed. Experienced managers often resist suggestions that they hire management consultants for this reason. "What can a consultant tell me that I don't already know?" is their common response. Governments in developing countries are sometimes reluctant to acknowledge publicly their reliance on foreign consultants since to do so might diminish the government's status in the eyes of the local population. As a result, a skilled advisor tries to maintain a low profile and avoids taking credit publicly for actions and decisions of a client. Inexperienced consultants sometimes cannot resist showing their knowledge and influence, and they occasionally lose their clients as a result. One American advisor who was working on a reform of the tax system in a West African country told many local officials and business executives that he was responsible for "determining the country's new tax policy." When reports of these conversations reached the Minister of Finance, he fired the American advisor.

Loss of Confidentiality

To operate effectively, an advisor needs information about the client and the first task is usually to secure that information. This transfer of information creates the risk that the client will lose confidentiality and that other people—competitors, enemies, and the general public—will obtain that information and use it to the detriment of the client. Thus an engineering consultant may gain access to a company's unpatented know-how and sell it to a competitor. Or a consulting psychologist may obtain knowledge of a patient's marital problems and reveal them to the patient's employer. Here, too, the experienced consultant must devise measures to assure the client of confidentiality.

Loss of Time

While the intervention of an advisor may slow down or stop a reckless act, it can also delay or obstruct a needed decision. Finding an advisor and obtaining advice is a time-consuming process that can in some cases become a justification for procrastination. Sometimes, however, the delays inherent in seeking advice can be advantageous. Political or business leaders faced with a difficult and contentious decision often use the device of seeking advisory opinions in order to avoid unpopular, but needed, decisions. In such situations, the advisory committee is often a favored device.

The advisor should be aware of the potential costs to the client and therefore manage their relationship in such a way as to minimize the costs and maximize the benefits.

SEVEN PRINCIPLES OF THE ART OF ADVICE

Managing the relationship of advisor and client for the benefit of both is an art—the art of advice. Like the arts of music, painting, or drama, the art of advice is governed by certain basic principles. There are in fact seven:

1. You must know your client. One of the great failings of oracle advisors is that they give advice without really understanding the people who will use it.

2. Help or at least do no harm. Following the injunction of Hippocrates to medical students, advisors should "help or at least do no harm." While it is true that no one can be forced to take advice, a person advising someone should realize that advice matters and can have serious consequences.

3. Agree on your role. Like an actor in a play or a musician in an orchestra, an advisor has a definite role to play in each advising situation, and the nature and scope of that role vary from case to case. But whereas an actor's role is defined by the playwright, the advisor's role is determined by negotiation between advisor and client.

4. Never give a solo performance. Oracles aside, advising is fundamentally a collaborative activity—a partnership between client and advisor. The advisor, then, is never a solo performer.

5. Play it clear and constructive. Advising is a process of individualized instruction. It must be tailored to the life, needs, and objectives of the client. But most of all, that process should be clear and constructive.

6. Keep your advice pure. Effectiveness of advice is always threatened by the advisor's own self-interest, prejudices, biases, and personal shortcomings. The challenge for the advisor is to keep advice free of these impurities.

7. Agree on the end at the beginning. In undertaking any artistic work, the artist must know when to stop—often the difference between a brilliant performance and a flawed one. The good advisor, too, must also recognize when advice is no longer needed or appropriate. Proper planning at the beginning of the advising relationship is the key to a good ending.

The seven rules of the art of advice, in the abstract, are short and simple. Their application in specific circumstances is often complex and difficult. Through experience, the skilled advisor learns how to apply these rules in a variety of situations and with a diversity of clients. The ineffective advisor does not. Let's now examine each of these rules in detail so that you can learn to master the art of advice.

2

KNOW
YOUR
CLIENT

**"It is an infallible rule that a
prince who is not wise himself
cannot be well advised."**
—Machiavelli, *The Prince*

LIKE THE ACTRESS WHO GAUGES HER AUDIENCE from the moment she steps on stage, the advisor must first know the client.
Knowing whether your client is a wise or a foolish prince will
tell you how to counsel him, or indeed, whether to advise him
at all. Although this rule may seem obvious, advisors often
fail to respect it. As a result, they sometimes end up like
chamber musicians mistakenly booked to play at a rock con-
cert—ignored, scorned, or hooted from the stage.

Knowing your client is important for two reasons—one
concerns *what* advice you give and the other affects *how* you
give it. The first is about substance, the second is about process.

Good advice must always meet your client's needs and circumstances, and your client is usually the best source of that
information. A financial counselor cannot create an effective

estate plan for a widow without knowing her income, expenses, lifestyle, family relationships, and assets. An auto salesman cannot really advise a customer on a car without knowing the customer's family size, driving habits, and commuting needs. A doctor cannot treat a pitcher's sore shoulder without first examining him, reviewing his medical history, and taking X rays. The client, then, is an important resource for the advisor—a source of information, ideas, and advice itself. The effective advisor taps that resource fully.

A second reason for knowing your client concerns the advising process itself—the way you go about giving advice. The effective advisor shapes the advising process to fit the client's abilities and background. To do that, you must know the client. The better a financial advisor knows the widow, the better the advisor can help her to evaluate financial options and make investment decisions that meet her needs. If the widow is an experienced businesswoman with an MBA from Harvard, an advisor can assume that she knows the difference between a stock and a bond, understands how financial markets work, and recognizes the importance of tax laws in making investment decisions. If, on the other hand, the widow never worked outside the home and left money matters to her husband, the advisor would need to spend a lot of time explaining the basics of personal finance before getting down to the merits of one mutual fund over another. Similarly, an American management consultant might be direct and blunt in giving advice to a group of U.S. executives but would need to be more circumspect in advising Japanese managers because of their cultural aversion to confrontation and public criticism. In short, both the advice and the advising process need to be tailored to the client's particular circumstances.

Effective advising requires a good working relationship between advisor and client. It is a relationship of mutual trust and confidence. That relationship can only develop if the advisor and the client know something about each other.

BARRIERS BETWEEN ADVISOR AND CLIENT

If the first rule of the art of advice is so obvious, why do so many advisors seem to ignore it so often? In fact, few advisors expressly deny the importance of getting to know their clients. In most instances, they genuinely believe that they know their clients well—or at least well enough to do their job. Often, however, they fail to gain that knowledge because of hidden barriers that exist between advisor and client—barriers like reefs beneath the sea that are usually discovered only after the advising relationship has crashed against them. Often the client builds these barriers, but sometimes it is the advisor who erects them. Let's examine the barriers that prevent an advisor from knowing a client and then see how they may be removed to allow the art of advice to flourish.

BARRIERS CREATED BY ADVISORS

Advisors unintentionally create barriers against their clients for many reasons. Three of the most common barriers are those arising from advisors' false assumptions, ego, and limited time.

Barriers from False Assumptions

An advisor's false assumptions about the client or the client's situation are the most frequent barriers that come between advisors and clients. Instead of determining all the facts, advisors often incorrectly assume that a particular situation exists, or they exclude an area from scrutiny because it does not seem relevant. For example, the president of an American corporation experiencing sluggish sales in the United States asked a management consultant to provide the company with a strategy for expansion into the European Community. After several months' work, the consultant gave the firm an elaborate plan for penetrating Europe, but the corporation never implemented it. In fact, management hardly considered it at all. The consultant had assumed the company was genuinely able and willing to increase its international markets. In reality, the company's sluggish sales at home and its drive for expansion abroad were caused by organizational difficulties and personal conflicts that were wracking corporate headquarters in Milwaukee. The company's president thought expansion into Europe would solve his problems, and the management consultant based his work on false assumptions about the needs and circumstances of the client. To know the client, an advisor should take very little for granted.

Making assumptions about clients is tempting for advisors. For one thing, assumptions seem to save time, effort, and money. They reduce the need to make painstaking, lengthy studies and examinations of the client. So the management consultant working on an international strategy for the Milwaukee company mentioned above did not waste time on studying corporate headquarters and instead got on with the job of figuring out how to get the company into the European Community. Time, after all, is the advisor's most precious resource—a resource that remains fixed no matter how hard the advisor works.

Ironically, an experienced advisor is sometimes more apt to make false assumptions than a new consultant is. The experience of having seen similar problems many times before can lull an experienced advisor into believing that superficial similarities between past situations and a current assignment mean that the essence of the problem is the same. So a financial advisor may invariably recommend mutual funds to middle-income couples, and a burned-out high school guidance counselor may automatically steer minority students from the inner city toward trade school and white students from the suburbs toward college.

The advisor comes to see a client as a specific type of problem rather than as a unique individual in a particular circumstance with a special set of needs, resources, and desires. Through sheer routine, the advisor becomes like an assembly line worker who attaches the same component to each auto chassis that passes his way. But while the assembly line always brings the auto worker identical chassis, life rarely, if ever, brings the advisor identical clients. Whether an advisor is a doctor or lawyer, a management consultant or a policy planner, it is important to remember that each client is unique.

The very act of failing to treat the client as unique can cause clients to react by raising barriers of their own against their advisors. Every client wants to be recognized as special—as one of a kind, not one of a class. A few years ago, an American management consultant was helping an African government reorganize its civil service. From the day of his arrival, he continually pointed out to various officials how their country's administrative problems were just like those he had successfully worked on in India. As he persisted in making this comparison, his African clients became cooler and less open toward him because they felt he was not recognizing the special nature of their country and its problems. As he detected the African officials' growing reserve, the advisor assumed it was caused by their uncertainty about his knowledge and experience, and he therefore mistakenly tried to counter it by reemphasizing his experience in India—a tactic that alienated his African clients even more. In the end, with his recommendations ignored and his access to high officials restricted, his consulting firm realized that he was totally frozen out of the administrative reform process, and it therefore decided to transfer him to another country six months before the end of his contract.

All advisors value their experience, and many consider it their most important asset. But an advisor's previous experience can be both helpful and misleading. It may give important lessons for solving the problem at hand or it may create barriers that prevent an advisor from seeing the client's reality. The experienced advisor therefore should remember Mark Twain's advice: "We should be careful to get out of an experience only the wisdom that is in it—and stop there; lest we be like the cat that sits down on a hot stove-lid. She will never sit down on a hot stove-lid again—and that is well; but also she will never sit down on a cold one any more."*

The Barriers of Ego and Power

The advisor's own ego and desires for status and power can also create barriers to knowing the client. By their language, their surroundings, and their behavior, advisors, either intentionally or unconsciously, often seek to establish a superior position over their clients. They are afflicted, one might say, with an oracle syndrome. Like the oracles of ancient times, these advisors are accessible only under certain conditions,

---

*Following the Equator. Pudd'nhead Wilson's New Calendar, reprinted in The Portable Mark Twain (de Voto, ed), p. 562.

speak a technical language that only other oracles can understand, and ensconce themselves in palatial office buildings that look like temples. They behave in this way for a variety of reasons—to show their superior knowledge, to control the client, or merely to copy what they think other advisors do. Whatever the reason, the effect of the oracle syndrome is to intimidate the client. An intimidated client is usually a defensive client, and a defensive person is not easy to know. In effect, by assuming behavior and trappings of an oracle, an advisor creates barriers that obstruct knowing the client. Virtually all advisors plan their offices, carry on their conversations, and conduct themselves in ways that they think will impress their clients. Only the wisest stop to ask themselves whether a massive mahogany desk, a penchant for technical jargon, and a condescending manner will hinder them in getting to know their clients, and therefore prevent them from doing a good job.

The Barrier of Limited Time

Time is a precious commodity for any advisor. The busy advisor is always tempted to shortchange a client on time. By rigidly limiting the time devoted to a client, the advisor creates a self-imposed barrier to knowing the client.

Realizing that work expands to fill the time that is given to it, the wise advisor also recognizes that giving too much time to a client can be wasteful and inefficient. Nonetheless, it is also helpful for an advisor to recognize that insufficient time can cause barriers in many respects. First, insufficient time may prevent the advisor from gathering all the information necessary to give good advice. Second, when an advisor gives insufficient time to a client, he or she is sending a message that the client is not very important, a message that in most cases will provoke a negative reaction. On the other hand, all clients have a tendency to assume that they and their problems deserve unlimited time from their advisors. The wise advisor must strike a balance between these two extremes. The test for determining how much time to devote to a client is whether the time is adequate or insufficient to help solve the client's problem. For example, a professor at a college, after several years' experience, believed that a half hour was ample time to advise students on selecting their courses for the year, so he rigidly established his advising schedule in half-hour intervals. Some students felt rushed by this process. For them, a discussion of career options had to precede any consideration of individual courses, and the professor simply did not allow enough time for this kind of discussion.

BARRIERS CREATED BY CLIENTS

Clients, too, can create barriers that prevent their advisors from knowing them. They do so because they have interests to protect in addition to their goal of obtaining help from their advisors. More specifically, client barriers are those of ego, self-interest, and time.

First, clients, like everybody else, protect their own egos, status, and sense of self-esteem. As a result, they are often reluctant to give information that they think will diminish their status in the eyes of their advisors. The CEO who wanted advice about entering the European Community did not reveal the discontent at headquarters, since that information might have tended to reduce the consultant's estimation of the CEO as a dynamic and effective leader. For the same reason, a patient may be reluctant to tell his doctor how much he is smoking, and a politician may be unwilling to reveal to her lawyer that she has taken a bribe. To overcome the barriers of ego, status, and self-esteem present in your client, you have to understand how the client perceives him- or herself and recognize the important elements of that self-perception. A client may also be unwilling to reveal information that will harm his or her interests. Accused thieves will not admit their crimes to their lawyers out of a fear that the information will be used against them. And a patient may fail to tell her doctor about persistent heartburn because she is afraid it may lead to an operation, unpleasant treatments, and restrictions on her diet and activities. Indeed, one woman steadfastly refused to be weighed during her annual physical examination in order to prevent her doctor from trying to advise her to lose weight.

Just as time is scarce for the advisor, it can also be in short supply for the client. One often has the image of the client waiting in the outer office to see a doctor, lawyer, or consultant. But it sometimes happens that the advisor must wait to see the client. Advisors to presidents, company CEOs, and government officials often have to adjust their advising techniques to their client's busy schedules. No client ends all other activities because he or she consults an advisor. As a result, the amount of time that a client may devote to an advisor is limited, and such limited time can create an obstacle for the advisor to come to know the client. The effective advisor seeks to understand and adjust to the constraints that time places upon the client. For example, skilled advisors to presidents, governors, and CEOs quickly learn to adjust their styles to a fundamental rule of bureaucratic life: Short memos are read first and brief statements impress most. Accordingly, they restrain the impulse of many experts to overwhelm others with their knowledge, and instead hone their presentation to the essential elements that will help clients with their problems.

BREAKING DOWN BARRIERS TO YOUR CLIENT

The effective advisor often has to break down barriers in order to know the client. One of the most powerful tools for dismantling a client barrier is the question. Knowing the right questions to ask is crucial for getting to know your client. In most cases where an advisor has made a false assumption about a client, it is because the advisor failed to ask the right question. The management consultant who accepted at face value the CEO's statements about the company's need to enter the European Community made false assumptions about the company's goals because he never asked *why* the company wanted to expand to Europe. The burned-out high school guidance counselor who automatically directed minority students to trade schools instead of college also made false assumptions about student aptitude and motivation. He did not take the time to ask individual students about their own particular goals, talents, and backgrounds. So the question is the advisor's basic tool. Here are a few fundamental questions that advisors should carry in their tool kits.

The Advisor's Instrumental Questions

The first question for any advisor encountering a person who seems to want advice is:

Do I Have a Client?

Your best friend comes by your office to tell you about a problem that she is having at work with two of her employees who refuse to cooperate. Your son calls on the telephone to tell you that he and his wife have had an argument over money and that he has moved out of the house. Your boss takes you to lunch and describes the conflict she is having with the finance department over her request for an increase in the operating budget for next year. In each case, your instinct is to offer these individuals advice with their problems. You care about each of them. In a very real sense, their success or happiness affects your own well-being. They like and respect you. They seem to be looking to you for help. If you fail to help, not only will their problems continue, but you may lose their respect. After all, if they can't get help from you—a trusted friend, devoted parent, loyal employee—where will they find it?

Before assuming the role of advisor, you should ask yourself a first and fundamental question: Do I have a client? Are your friend, your son, and your boss really asking you for advice? Or do they just want to express their feelings and tell you their troubles? In short, do they want wise counsel or simply a sympathetic ear? An experienced advisor recognizes that there is a great difference between asking for advice and asking for understanding. Before you become an advisor, it is important to understand what exactly your friend, son, or boss wants from you. Do not assume that persons who tell you their troubles want you to be their advisor. They may definitely not want advice, or they may not be sure they want advice. Unless they want your advice, don't give it. You don't have a client. With time, that situation may change as a person thinks about the problem and looks for possible sources of help.

Which One Is My Client?

The question may seem simple to answer: My client is the person who asks my advice. That answer is correct in most cases where a single individual is seeking your advice. But if organizations or a group of persons want your advice, determining who precisely your client is may not be so easy. A veterinarian once summed up the problem succinctly: "When I first began to practice, I thought my patient was just the animal. Now I know it's both the animal and the owner."

For example, if the president of the company asks you to prepare a consulting report on the company's ability to absorb new technologies, is your client the president, the board of directors, or the whole company? Legally, your client is the company. It is the company who is paying you; it is the company with which you have a contractual relationship. The president is dealing with you as the company's agent or representative. On the other hand, it is the president who defines your mission and whom you must ultimately satisfy. So as a practical matter, you may have two clients. As long as their interests are the same, your relationship with the two will go smoothly. If their interests diverge, you may face the difficult task of responding to your primary client and thereby earn the anger of your secondary client. For example, if you find that the president's management style reduces the company's ability to absorb new technologies, your duty to the company will require you to deal with the problem in your report.

A similar situation can arise when an advisor is seeking to help a child, and the parent is paying the fee. Inevitably, the advisor must satisfy both the parent and the child, but the primary client is the child, and it is the child's interests that must predominate. But for the advisor, whether counseling on suitable colleges or effective ways to treat acne, it is important to remember that both child and parent have to be dealt with, communicated to, and understood. In many situations, the great challenge for an advisor is to give the right advice to the primary client, such as the company or the child, and yet to do it in such a way that the secondary client, like the company president or the parent, will understand and accept it.

What Is My Client Like?

Once you have identified your clients, you then have to get to know who they are. Each client brings to the advisor a past, a present, and a desired future, and the advisor needs to know all three. The past consists of the events and history that have influenced the client's situation today: for example, the growth of a West Coast computer company from its founding in a garage in Palo Alto, the medical history of a sick old man from his birth in a poor area of rural Poland, or the background of a homeowner threatened with a mortgage foreclosure by a bank. The client's present is the current situation—problems and factors that have led to a search for help. The computer company's decline in sales, the old man's pain in the lower back, and the threatened lawsuit facing a debtor are the factors of the present that have led the client to get help from the advisor. And finally, every client, whether it is a troubled computer company, a limping patient, or a harassed homeowner, has a desired future that they hope the advisor will help them to attain. It is important for the advisor to know and understand that contemplated future—the client's hoped-for objectives.

The past, the present, and the future give the advisor a tripartite format for getting to know the client. Until you have gathered this information about the client's past, present, and future, you cannot know him or her. And until you know the client, you cannot do an effective job. For example, suppose that a charitable organization has asked for your advice on the design of its newsletter. The inexperienced advisor may be tempted to come to the first meeting with an assortment of attractive designs and formats. The experienced advisor, on the other hand, knows that no design can serve the client unless the designer has an understanding of the organization's past, present, and future. Even if the charity wants a new image that breaks completely with its stodgy past, the designer needs to understand the stodgy past in order to prepare designs for a brilliant future. At the same time, the advisor needs to know the organization's current situation and capability. And finally, the advisor needs to know the charity's objectives: just what does it want to achieve with a restyled newsletter?

A client is therefore like a traveler. Any advisor, whether a doctor or lawyer, consulting engineer or financial planner, needs to get answers to the three traveler's questions to really know the client: (1) Where have you been? (2) Where are you now? (3) Where do you want to go?

Simply asking the three questions will not get you the information you need. Indeed, if you did ask these exact questions bluntly, your client is likely to become confused, cautious, or even hostile. As a result, you will get less, not more, information. The three questions are simply guides that you should follow in getting to know your client. For example, you will ordinarily have to ask many questions just to know where your client has been.

Sometimes it may be wiser to ask no questions at all but to use other forms of communication to encourage your client to talk. A shy teenage clerk in your store hesitantly comes into your office. He is obviously troubled, but is having difficulty talking to you. Rather than asking him directly, "What is your problem?"—a question that can be confrontational—you may obtain more information simply by saying, "So you seem to be having a problem"—a statement that invites further comment and implies that having problems is normal and natural. How you phrase your questions and statements and toward what particular events they will be directed will depend on the kind of advisor you are, the kind of client you have, and the kind of problem you hope to solve. Sometimes advisors need to help the client determine objectives. Indeed, deciding on future objectives may be precisely the problem that the client is struggling with. Or the client's stated objective, upon examination, may turn out to be inappropriate. For example, suppose a young executive asks your advice about changing jobs. Before you begin suggesting people to contact, you would be wise to find out why the executive wants to change her job. It may well be that she has decided to quit because of some difficulties in her current work situation—for example, a domineering boss—and that dealing with that precise problem—say, a transfer within the company—might resolve the matter without the need to look for another job.

The depth and breadth of your inquiry have to be guided by two factors: *relevance* to the nature of the problem and *proportionality* to its importance. If General Motors seeks your advice on how best to enter the markets of the former Soviet Union, a complete history of the company since its founding would be more than you need or want to know about your client. However, it would be useful to know about previous dealings in the Soviet Union and other relevant foreign transactions. Thus the advisor must seek information that is relevant and that is helpful in assisting the client. Similarly, making a vast historical study would require time and expense that is out of proportion to the task one is asked to undertake. Relevance and proportionality, then, are the standards that will guide the task of getting to know your client.

CAN WE TALK?

For nearly all advisors, the primary mechanism for getting to know the client is the interview. Physicians read the patient's medical history. Lawyers examine the client's file. Management consultants read company financial statements. But none of these documents is as important for getting to know the client as the face-to-face meeting is. It is through conversation between advisor and client that the three questions are answered and the advisor truly comes to know the client.

The skill with which the advisor conducts the interview is crucial. It is at the interview that useful information is gathered and valuable insights gained or that barriers are created and false assumptions made. The interview is a very serious matter, and commentators from various professions always treat it in weighty terms. But the interview can also be viewed as a game, a game whose outcome depends not only on the advisor's choices but on the client's choices as well. As in any game, both advisor and client consciously or subconsciously are trying to anticipate probable future moves of the other side. The game may be cooperative or it may become competitive, a game of catch or a football game. In playing the interview game, the advisor needs to keep several strategic factors in mind.

Your Place or Mine?

First, where will the interview take place? In many cases, it will take place in the office of the advisor. Consequently, the advisor should consider how best to create an environment that will allow the advisor to come to know the client early and well.

Advisors often design their offices to impress or even overwhelm their clients. The rugs are thick, the furniture is plush, and the view is spectacular. While these surroundings may convey the advisor's wealth and status, they may at the same time discourage the client from talking freely. Much, of course, depends on who the client is. A corporation president may feel perfectly comfortable in discussing his marital problems in a divorce lawyer's opulent office with a view of San Francisco Bay, but a battered sixteen-year-old wife will probably be considerably less at ease in talking about her marriage in these surroundings. Advisors should therefore try to remain aware of how their offices will affect their clients' willingness and ability to make themselves known to their advisors. For many advisors a big desk is a symbol of status and power, but it can also communicate messages to the client that inhibit communication. The advisor who wants to put the client at ease to encourage conversation may find it useful to get out from behind the desk and to hold the interview in a sitting area off to one side or in a comfortable, less imposing conference room.

In many cases, it may be to the advisor's advantage to meet the client on the client's territory. That territory—the client's office or factory, the people who work there, the pictures on the walls—may tell much about the client that can help the advisor to get to know the client. One experienced lawyer who plans wills and estates always makes at least one "house call" to a client's home because it helps him to know the client better. In still other situations, a wise advisor may try to get the client on neutral territory to conduct the interview by going for a walk in the park or having a cup of coffee at a quiet restaurant. One Boston consultant often invites a new client to attend a Red Sox game with him. The appropriate surroundings can ease a client's tension and lower defenses between client and advisor.

Who Should Play?

A second major consideration is to decide who should be at the interview. The number and types of persons can encourage or inhibit conversation at the crucial stage when the advisor is trying to know the client. It is important to determine who should attend the interview from both the advisor's and the client's side. In order to demonstrate their resources, status, or prestige, advisors will often have members of the staff attend the meetings that are designed to get to know the client. For example, a lawyer might ask a paralegal or an associate to be present at a meeting. On the one hand, if the associate or paralegal is to work on the client's problem, their presence saves time. On the other hand, a client may feel intimidated in direct proportion to the number of people in the room and thereby become guarded in conversation. A similar judgment has to be made with respect to the client's attendance at the meeting. While a single person may have approached the advisor for help, it may become apparent that the advisor needs to know other people—a spouse or a parent—in order to get to know the client.

In cases where a client is an organization, the advisor has to determine which people in that organization should be interviewed so that the advisor can get to know it. For example, if your client is a multinational Swiss manufacturing corporation, the central bank of an Asian country, or a nonprofit social welfare agency in California, whom should you interview among literally thousands of officers and employees in order to come to know your client? Here, too, the principles of relevance and proportionality apply. You have to make careful judgments about the persons able to give you relevant information and about the amount of your time and effort that is proportionate to the significance of the problem on which you are working. When an organization is your client, you risk becoming a "captive advisor" of one or a few persons who seek to be your principal source of information. Those very individuals may be the problem, but you may never know it until you gain other information sources. On the other hand, if you spend all your time getting to know the organization, you may never be able to help solve the problem.

In one case, an American professor received a sixty-day assignment to advise an African central bank on improving procedures for reviewing loans made by the country's commercial banks. He spent the entire two months interviewing virtually all of the bank's employees and reading all of the bank's annual reports since its founding. At the end of his assignment, he submitted a report recommending a yearlong study of the bank's structure and operations and arguing against any change in lending regulations until the bank corrected all of its organizational and "systemic" problems. The governor of the central bank angrily rejected the report and protested to the professor's employer that the consultant had failed to complete his assignment. Ultimately, the consulting organization that employed the professor had to agree with the governor. While the professor may have had a sound theoretical basis for his recommendation, the time he already spent and still wanted to spend on getting to know his client was totally out of proportion to the problem he was asked to solve and the resources that the client could afford to devote to it.

When Should We Talk?

An advisor must not only decide how much time to devote to interviews but also *when* those interviews should take place. In scheduling interviews, you should carefully consider surrounding events that might interfere with or negatively influence the meeting and reduce its effectiveness as an opportunity to get to know your client. For example, a friend of your daughter, whom you have never met, calls to ask for a meeting to get your advice about a company that has made her a job offer. She is supposed to meet with the company vice-president next Wednesday afternoon to discuss salary and precise job responsibilities. If possible, you should try to meet her before Wednesday to give you the time to get to know her and to explore unanticipated issues. She is likely to be more relaxed and open with you on Monday afternoon than on Wednesday morning, when the impending meeting will undoubtedly dominate her thoughts.

What Are the Rules of the Game?

The objective of the interview is to allow the advisor to get to know the client so as to help solve a particular problem. To play that game to maximum advantage, an advisor needs to follow a few important rules:

1. Let your clients get to know you. A relationship of trust and confidence is built on the idea of mutuality. If you let your clients come to know you, your clients will be encouraged to let you know them. A doctor should not assume that his white coat, the stethoscope around his neck, and the medical diplomas on the wall tell patients all they need to know. Information about the doctor as a person will encourage the patient to talk more freely. Like a game of catch, if you want your partner to throw the ball to you, you have to be prepared to throw the ball to your partner.

2. Let your clients tell their own stories in their own way. To know your clients, you have to be prepared to let them tell you about themselves and their problems in their own way. Some advisors grow impatient with this approach. They feel that their clients ramble, waste time, and give irrelevant information. It is much easier to put them on the right track with a few leading questions—or even better, a pointed direction. The problem with this method is that the advisor, through false assumptions, may lead the client in the wrong direction. Advisors often try to control the client in the interview; the better approach is to let go.

3. Hang on your client's lips. In order to know your clients, you need to listen to them actively and empathetically. Through verbal and nonverbal signs, you must assure them that you are hearing what they have to say, that you sympathize with their situation. The nineteen-century novelist Anthony Trollope described Lucy Morris, a character who had the great ability to listen empathetically and to encourage people to talk, as "hanging on their lips." The good advisor hangs on the lips of his or her client. In practice, this means that the advisor encourages the client to talk through nods, eye contact, and words of encouragement. Sometimes when you are faced with a reticent client, merely repeating the client's last statement will stimulate further conversation. Hanging on your clients' lips also means concentrating carefully on what they are saying. In this endeavor, all advisors must struggle against distractions—sounds outside the room, thoughts about your next meeting, regrets about your last interview. For many advisors, a major distraction stems from what the client is saying. What the client is saying can be a distraction if it causes the advisor to try to anticipate the client's statements and to guess where the client is heading in his or her narrative. The effective advisor patiently lets the client tell the story and avoids racing on ahead.

4. Don't interrupt. The authoritative advisor sometimes asserts authority by interrupting the client when he is talking. The advisor has heard enough to know the problem, so why waste time while the client drones on? It is always bad practice for the advisor to interrupt the client. For one thing, the advisor may be assuming that she knows enough when, in fact, there is much more she could learn if only she would let the client talk. For another, a good working relationship between client and advisor is essential to a productive advising process. Constantly interrupting the client leads to a nonproductive relationship, one that is likely to provoke the client's resentment and frustration.

5. Don't talk too soon. Inexperienced advisors, anxious to prove their value to their clients, often start giving advice before they fully know the client or the problem. They seem to feel that they will lose the client's respect unless they show what they know. But talking about the substance of the client's problem before you know the client can lead to bad advice. Therefore, you should avoid talking about substance until you feel that the client has given you all the necessary information.

6. Put yourself in your client's shoes. An advisor needs to listen with empathy and understanding. Listening empathetically is not just a sham tactic to encourage your client to talk. Real empathy will allow you to understand the client and the problem well; with that understanding, creative problem solving can begin. One of the best ways to gain empathy for the client is to try to put yourself in the client's place, to try to see and feel the problem from the client's perspective.

7. Pay attention to nonverbal communication. Clients communicate by actions as well as words. Some anthropologists estimate that 60 percent of all communication is nonverbal. In fact, most important emotional messages—like those conveying friendship or anger, confidence or mistrust—are expressed nonverbally by gestures, facial expressions, or tone of voice. As a result, the advisor must know how to read the client's nonverbal communications during the interview. For example, the client who leans far back in the chair with arms crossed may be signaling his lack of confidence in the advisor.

8. Don't be judgmental. During the interview, an advisor should avoid making judgments on what the client is saying. Nonjudgmental understanding encourages clients to talk freely. A client who senses that an advisor is judgmental will be tempted to tell her story in a way that will gain the advisor's approval or at least avoid implied criticism. As a result, the advisor will not get the full story and therefore will face a barrier in getting to know the client. For example, an abused wife seeking help from a counselor is not likely to speak freely if early in the interview the counselor asks: "How could you marry a person like that?" Similarly, you should avoid at all costs responding to your clients' tales of woe with the usual admonition, "If only you had come to see me sooner. . . ." Other than serving to praise your own abilities, that statement makes a negative judgment on how your clients manage their affairs, and it will invariably cause clients to become defensive and guarded in their relations with you.

These eight rules will help you to know your clients, but gaining that knowledge is only the first step in the advising process. We now need to see how that knowledge can be put to work to help clients solve their problems.

3

HELP,
OR AT LEAST
DO NO HARM

"As to diseases, make a habit
of two things—to help, or at
least to do no harm."
—Hippocrates, *Epidemics I*

ADVISING IS HELPING. All clients, no matter how powerful,
need help. They need help because they are in some way
deficient. They lack the necessary knowledge, ideas, perspec-
tives, confidence, or time to accomplish a desired task.
Whether they are presidents of countries or seniors in college,
clients seek advisors precisely because they feel that they can
pursue their goals better with the help of good advice than they
can without it. If your clients did not sense some deficiency in
themselves, they would not bother to ask your advice.

Overwhelmed by the pressures of office and the demands of
many special interests, a president needs the objective counsel
of trusted advisors to help in choosing cabinet officers, shaping
foreign policy, and deciding on bills to send to Congress.
Faced with a business world that they barely know, college
seniors look to experienced executives for help in deciding on

a career. In both cases, the advisor's role is to help the client to do something better than he or she would do alone. For an advisor, then, helping means improving a client's performance—whether the task is choosing a good secretary of the treasury or finding the best way to get into the advertising business.

An important first step in helping is to understand precisely in what way the client is deficient. What is it that your clients lack to do the jobs for which they seek advice? The answer to that question will vary from client to client and from situation to situation. In some cases, the client needs the advisor's knowledge to remedy the deficiency. In other cases, the client has that knowledge and therefore holds the means to solve the problem. Sometimes the best help an advisor can give is not to offer learned opinions but rather to confirm the client's own ideas and to strengthen the client's confidence in his or her own judgment. The college senior who asks advice from an experienced executive about career options may already have gathered much information about the advertising business. What the student needs most is not more information but assurance that his approach to looking for a job with an advertising agency is a good one. On the other hand, a cancer patient trying to decide between surgery, chemotherapy, and radiation as treatments needs help in understanding probable outcomes and results, the likely advantages and disadvantages that each option may offer.

Clients' principal deficiencies include:

1. Lack of information. A client may simply not have sufficient information to do a particular task. A recently widowed woman may not have an adequate knowledge of stocks and bonds to invest her inheritance, so she will turn to an advisor for help. Confronted with several new communications systems, a company will hire a consultant to assist in choosing the right one for its line of business.

2. Lack of analysis or insight. A client may have an abundance of information but may be unable to interpret it in a meaningful way. A CEO of a declining textile business knows all the facts and figures about his company and its markets but cannot interpret them to understand just what is happening to his business and what he should do about it. An experienced management consultant can help the CEO analyze the situation and develop a new strategy.

3. Lack of confidence. A client may have formed an idea of what to do about a problem, but may feel the need for independent advice to confirm his or her views. Sometimes when a client is under great stress, the best help an advisor can give is to provide emotional support to the client confronting difficult choices. Rulers facing decisions about war and peace have often sought the emotional support of their advisors.

4. Lack of time. For many clients, a primary deficiency in making a decision or doing a task is a lack of time. With enough time, they often have the ability to gather the information and make the analysis needed for a good decision. Since their other obligations prevent them from devoting enough time to a task, they turn to advisors for help.

5. Lack of will. Clients sometimes lack the will to take actions that they know are right. A governor has great difficulty denying requests by supporters for favors that are not in the public interest. A company president finds it painful to cut departmental budgets or order the layoff of workers. Often, in cases like these, the advisor's role is to strengthen clients' resolve—

to get them to do the right thing. Alone, the governor might grant the favor against her better judgment. Backed by her advisor, she finds the strength to say no.

A particular client may be deficient in more than one of these ways. The skilled advisor will determine precisely the nature of the deficiency and proceed to offer help accordingly. Advisors sometimes lose sight of the fact that they exist to help the client. Often they come to see clients as existing to serve the interests of the advisor. Advisors to presidents and kings sometimes think the purpose of their job is not to help, but rather to advance their own power and prestige. In Shakespeare's play *Othello*, Iago, for example, pursued his own interests by manipulating Othello. Advisors to powerful people often give advice in a way that assures that they will not lose their influence with the presidents and kings they serve. That kind of advice may not really help the client. Even advisors to friends may place their friendship above the need to give helpful advice, particularly when that advice may cause pain.

During the Vietnam War, advisors and friends of Lyndon Johnson kept assuring him of his popularity in the United States, despite widespread public protests against him. As the 1968 presidential election approached, they all urged him to seek reelection. One advisor, however, injected a note of hard reality into the discussions when he said, "You can run, Mr. President, and you will almost certainly win. But the only places you will be able to campaign are Fort Bragg and the aircraft carrier *Enterprise*." Ultimately, Johnson chose not to run.

BAD NEWS BEARERS

Telling a client bad news is a test of an advisor's commitment to helping. No advisor likes to give clients bad news—to tell a patient that she has AIDS, to inform a prisoner that he has lost an appeal, to tell the president that his popularity has fallen. At the very least, this kind of news will cause the client pain and provoke emotional reactions that the advisor must deal with. More seriously, the client may blame the advisor for the bad news and therefore the future relationship between advisor and client may become troubled. To avoid these risks, the weak or unscrupulous advisor may delay or minimize bad news or even find a justification not to give it at all.

Effective advisors know that they have to tell their clients unpleasant facts in order to be of real help. Making clients aware of bad news can be an essential first step in allowing them to improve their performance. The AIDS patient must understand her condition in order to begin treatment. A president must first know about influence peddling by his relatives in order to protect himself from scandal. Recognition that a company has lost market share is the first step for management to devise a new strategy to regain customers. Powerful clients often have difficulty in learning bad news. Advisors to kings and presidents do not like to tell their clients bad news because they fear they will lose influence. Advisors who make a habit of delivering bad news sometimes lose more than that. They lose their jobs. In centuries past, they might also have lost their heads.

A president or CEO who has several advisors may find it particularly hard to learn bad news. Often advisors compete with one another for their client's attention, and an advisor who delivers bad news once too often can lose out in that competition. In the struggle for influence among advisors, the goal of helping the president gets lost. Advisors therefore withhold information rather than risk a loss of favor with their clients. Helping the client in many cases demands not only knowledge and skill from the advisor but also courage.

Obviously, the way in which you deliver bad news to your client is important. Remember that your goal is to help the client so that he or she may act to improve his or her situation. Unwelcome information that is delivered in an insensitive manner can brutalize a client and therefore make remedial action difficult.

When you need to deliver bad news to a client, you will be most helpful if you keep these three rules in mind:

1. Prepare your delivery ahead of time. To deliver bad news, you must know your client well. You must know the client's strengths, weaknesses, and likely ways of coping with the news once it is received. You should prepare your delivery accordingly. If you anticipate your client's reaction will be denial, you should be prepared to present the facts calmly and to discuss them at length. You should also understand your own feeling about the bad news you are delivering. Since most advisors by the very nature of the relationship are close to their clients, bad news for the client is usually bad news for the advisor.

2. Plan the timing and context. Proper planning of the timing and context for delivery of bad news is crucially important. These factors may be the difference between a client who is devastated and fatalistic and one who is prepared to act to improve a difficult situation. Some moments are better than others for delivering bad news, and the effective advisor knows the best time to make a delivery. For example, a political advisor to a candidate for the U.S. Senate would prefer to tell the client about an adverse opinion poll after, rather than just before, an important campaign debate, so as not to weaken the candidate's confidence.

The context and setting for telling your client unwelcome information can be equally important. Generally, a face-to-face meeting with the client is a better setting for giving bad news than a telephone call or letter, and you should be sure that the two of you will have ample time to talk about the news without interruptions.

3. Have a proposal for action. You should meet your client with a plan of action or a list of options on how to deal with the bad news. Upon hearing the bad news, the client will immediately look to you for help, and you must be ready to offer it. For example, the most recent opinion polls show that your candidate's popularity is falling. You should not only deliver the bad news but also set out ways to turn the situation around. In one case, a young man named Tom accepted a job with a specific promise that he would stay at least a year with the firm. After two months, he found that he was dissatisfied at work, but felt that he could not leave because of his promise. He consulted his minister about the right thing to do, and the minister told him that the morally right thing to do was to keep his promise. That was, of course, bad news for Tom. The minister did not stop there. He also proposed a plan of action. While it might be unethical to quit, it was not unethical for Tom to renegotiate his obligation with his employer and to offer to help find a replacement. So rather than quit or sulk, Tom talked with the firm manager, who readily agreed with the plan. In the end, Tom found a replacement and left the firm with a clear conscience. Thanks to the minister's advice, both Tom and the firm found a happy solution.

IF YOU CAN'T HELP, DON'T HURT

When Hippocrates advised Greek physicians "to help, or at least to do no harm," he knew that the practice of medicine had the capacity for both healing and injuring. Advising also has the potential for both helping and harming. Early in his presidency, John Kennedy relied on bad advice when he authorized the Bay of Pigs invasion, an event that badly shook his administration. The source of Kennedy's problem was that the advice he received came from a small group of officials. Later, after reorganizing and broadening the advisory system in the White House, he received sound advice that allowed him to deal effectively with the Cuban missile crisis so as to halt the Soviet military buildup in Cuba while avoiding a nuclear war.

Unskilled advisors sometimes fail to see that bad advice can cause their clients considerable damage. It is, after all, the client rather than the advisor who pays the price for bad advice. As President Kennedy once remarked, the advisor, after giving advice, goes on to other advice, but the official whom he advises goes on to an election. *

Each of us is ready with advice. We are flattered when friends, family, colleagues, and even strangers ask our counsel. Next to imitation, asking for advice probably is the sincerest form of flattery. It recognizes our knowledge and wisdom, so how can we refuse? As a result, out of love, friendship, or just plain pride, most of us readily respond to requests for advice

---

* Peter Szanton, *Not Well Advised* (New York: Russell Sage, 1981), p. 140.

on anything from buying a new car to selling an old house, from launching a career to planning a retirement. Sometimes we respond *too* readily. Sometimes we fail to recognize that the advice we give our friends and clients can have serious consequences on their lives.

Advice, whether paid for or free, is not just a lot of talk. Advice always matters, and bad advice can do a great deal of damage. For example, advice on business strategy can affect a company's operations and its employees for years to come. A broker's recommendation to a customer to buy limited partnership interests in oil drilling ventures can lead to serious financial injury when the well turns out to be dry and the Internal Revenue Service disallows the deduction of drilling costs on the customer's income tax return. Similarly, an offhand remark by an insurance adjuster that an injured road-accident victim has three years to sue can cause further harm for the victim when it later turns out that the victim could not begin a suit against the state since he had not filed a claim notice within a year of the accident.

A client, of course, is always free to reject advice. No one forced the stockbroker's customer to buy the limited partnership interest, and nobody prevented the accident victim from suing the state the day after the accident. Both people made their choices freely. Unfortunately, both choices turned out to be wrong.

The fact that a client is always free to reject advice does not relieve the advisor from the responsibility for the consequences of giving that advice in the first place. What advisors often fail to realize is that by virtue of their position they have *power* over the client. The basis of that power is the *reliance* that the client has placed on the advisor. The moment a client asks for advice, he or she is relying at least to some extent on the advisor. By relying on the advisor, the client is giving the advisor power over some part of the client's life.

By stopping to ask directions at a roadside stand in rural Massachusetts, a driver from New York is giving the stand owner the power to influence the next phase of the trip. By asking a management consultant to recommend a business strategy to enter the Japanese market, a company president is giving the consultant power to influence the firm's profitability, for better or for worse. Advisors have power over clients, and that power may grow as the relationship continues and the client's reliance on advice increases.

The image that most advisors like to project is that of wise, kind, and selfless helpers—people who work only in the interests of their clients, rather than people who wield power. Even when that image reflects reality, all well-intentioned advisors—whether a pipe-smoking professor counseling a student on courses or an aging uncle advising a nephew on a career—also have power over their clients by virtue of the advising relationship. Both advisor and client should realize that the advising relationship is also a power relationship.

It is this power that enables the advisor to help the client. But it is also this power that allows an advisor to advance his or her own interests. Advising is a means to influence other people. Like the processes of negotiation and advocacy, the process of advising can be used to influence decisions and policies. Consequently, advocates for a policy or parties interested in a decision sometimes try to assume the role of advisor to the person who will have to make that policy or decision. When the president of a midwestern university had to decide whether to close the sociology department, many faculty members suddenly emerged as advocates on one side or the other. A few, however, took a different approach: They attempted to influence the president's decision by seeking to become "advisors," by seeking to counsel the president on what he should do about closing the department. Some of the advisors may have had a sincere interest in helping, but others were really partisans in advisor's clothing.

The difference between approaching a conflict as an open advocate and becoming involved in the disguise of an advisor is the difference between going to war in uniform and going to war as an undercover agent behind enemy lines. Whereas decision makers can easily recognize an openly partisan advocate and judge such advocacy accordingly, decision makers failing to perceive a partisan in advisor's clothing may not evaluate the "advice" with appropriate skepticism. The primary difference between a partisan advocate and an partisan advisor is that the former has a interest in a given issue and makes that interest known to the decision maker. What makes partisan advisors so dangerous is that they also have an interest in the issue but hide that fact from the decision maker, a fact that is essential for accurate evaluations of the "advice" received by the client. As a result, it is important for any client, whether college president or college senior, to seek to understand the interests of individuals whom they would choose as their advisors.

It is safe to assume that all advisors have their own interests and that those interests, consciously or unconsciously, will shape the advice they give. The historian who recommends that the university president close down the sociology department may make strong academic arguments to justify that advice, but those arguments become less forceful once the president learns that the historian has been feuding with the head of the sociology department for the last ten years or that the history department is planning to ask for a portion of the sociology department's funding once it is closed. The effective and honest advisor is sensitive to his or her own interests in a particular case and reveals those interests to the client. The self-interested advisor is not the only one who can harm the client with advice. The well-intentioned but careless or ignorant advisor is just as dangerous. Your casual recommendation to a restless junior manager to "take a year off and see the world" may fulfill your own daydreams but stunt the career of the junior manager. Your offhand remark to an impressionable student that academic studies should not interfere with extracurricular activities may give the student exactly the excuse he needs for cutting classes and submitting late assignments. Before offering counsel, the effective advisor should try to determine the impact that the advice will have on the client. Specifically, will your advice help or will it harm the client? In order to answer this question, you must start by putting yourself in the place of the client.

SITTING IN THE CLIENT'S CHAIR

In most offices, there are chairs for advisors and chairs for clients. Advisors and clients rarely sit in each other's chairs. Similarly, advisors and clients establish a relationship with each other early in their association, and they may never stop to consider how they appear to each other. To be an effective advisor, you need to sit in your client's chair from time to time—figuratively, if not literally. You need to understand how the client's problem and its relationship with you looks from the client's chair. You will then gain a new understanding on how to help the client, and you will perhaps avoid moves that will do him or her harm. Through this process, the advisor to a company president will see the pressures on the president from the board of directors, creditors, suppliers, and top management, and she will come to understand why the president is so slow to implement recommended organizational changes. Similarly, a medical doctor will appreciate the fears, anxieties, and confusion of a patient who has just learned he has cancer and is trying to understand his options for treatment. Putting yourself in your clients' chair will allow you to understand the vulnerabilities and risks that they feel and the strengths and weaknesses that they bring to the advising process. With that knowledge, you will be able to give advice that is less likely to do harm than if you had steadfastly sat in the advisor's seat.

FORETELLING THE FUTURE

Clients seek advice to cope with the future. The cancer patient wants help in deciding on the best treatment to regain his health in the future. A college senior needs counsel to plan a future career. A president needs help in choosing cabinet members who will do a good job in the years ahead. What clients seek is not just help, but help with the future.

Advice is therefore a prediction about the future. Whether an advisor is a doctor or lawyer, a financial consultant or a psychotherapist, his or her mission is to help the client make a better future. Hippocrates' instruction to Greek physicians 2,500 years ago is equally applicable to advisors today: "Declare the past, diagnose the present, foretell the future."* For advisors today, the challenge of foretelling the future is as great as it was in Hippocrates' time. The uncertainty of prediction remains a trap that awaits all advisors. Will the person recommended for secretary of the treasury develop tight fiscal controls, or will he be overwhelmed by the incessant demands of

---

* Hippocrates, *Epidemics I.*

government departments for more money? Will the college senior prove to have the talent for advertising or would he have been better off going into accounting? Will the cancer patient be able to handle strong chemotherapy or should he have chosen radiation and surgery?

No advisor, no matter how experienced, can be certain of the future. The best that an advisor can do is to estimate the probability based on all the information available. It is for this reason that it is essential to know the client, since the client holds much of the information that will allow you to make a reasonable estimate of probabilities.

For all this talk about the uncertainty of the future, human beings tend to operate on the assumption that the future is largely predictable. True, we are often surprised by unexpected events—the breakup of the Soviet Union, Iraq's invasion of Kuwait, the stock market's fall in 1987. But for the most part, we plan our lives and businesses with the expectation that certain actions taken now will bring about expected results later. A corporate reorganization today will make the company more profitable two years from now. An improved diet and increased exercise will lead an invalid to better health in six months. An investment this year in a biomedical firm in Boston will yield a big capital gain half a decade from now. The role of the advisor is to help the client make each of these actions so as to achieve the desired results—to restructure the company, not destroy it; to prescribe a diet and exercise program for better health, not more pain and sickness; to select a biotech firm that will prosper, not go broke. Clients want an experienced advisor, instead of a novice, because they believe that the value of experience resides in its ability to give the advisor insights into the future. If experience had no utility for the future, an experienced advisor and an inexperienced novice would stand on equal footing and, incidentally, would deserve equal fees. The past, we believe, contains knowledge about the future.

As an advisor, you are therefore a futurologist. Your education and experience have taught you that there are certain patterns in life. Your knowledge of those patterns can help your client achieve certain desired results in the future. The problem, of course, is that while these patterns may be regular much of the time, they are also affected by unexpected or unseen forces and events.

To predict the future, advisors use a variety of techniques. Those techniques are helpful but they are by no means certain. The following are four of the more important techniques that advisors use to foretell the future for their clients.

Trend Projection

This technique assumes that certain trends that have been happening in the past will continue to happen, and that the duration and speed of those trends can be projected into the future. Thus specialists in world oil markets, detecting a growing demand for oil in the early 1970s, projected a trend of rising oil prices for the remainder of the decade. On the basis of that projection, they advised clients on investing in refineries and tankers. At the same time financial advisors projected growing inflation rates throughout the world and advised corporate clients to finance expansion through debt that could be paid off in cheaper dollars in the years ahead. Advisors of all types are constantly trying to identify trends and then to project them for the benefit of their clients. Thus a career counselor, noticing a pattern of growth in the advertising business, might conclude that employment opportunities in advertising will grow in the future. But simple projection of trends can become a trap, particularly if the advisor fails to see the emergence of forces and factors that may divert a trend or even stop it dead in its tracks. Many advisors in the late 1970s predicted that oil prices could only go higher and that the world could expect to buy oil for $100 a barrel within a few years. What these advisors failed to see, of course, was that increased oil prices would encourage widespread energy conservation and a major effort to find new sources of oil—both of which served to slow and eventually stop the trend of rising oil prices.

Analogical Forecasting

Another technique for predicting the future of a particular situation is to look for a similar situation in the past. We thus create an analogy between the prior event and what we think may happen in similar circumstances. A financial advisor sees a close similarity between current stock market conditions and those prevailing just before the 1929 crash, so he advises his clients to sell all their shares. A physician determines that a patient has all the symptoms of malaria cases that she has previously treated, so she advises the patient to follow treatment for malaria. A management consultant sees strong parallels between his current client and a corporation that successfully achieved profitability by divesting unrelated businesses, so he recommends a similar program of divestitures.

Analogies are important tools for the advisor. Generally speaking, the more experienced the advisor, the more analogies that he or she has to draw on. The principal trap in using this technique is to make sure that you are relying on the right past experience to formulate advice for a future action. Many times the analogy between the past and present situation will seem identical, but the analogy fails to give good guidance because the advisor did not see important distinguishing characteristics between earlier experiences and the case at hand. As a result, the market does not crash as it did in 1929, the patient proves not to have malaria, and the program of divestments fails to increase the company's profitability. Analogical forecasting is an important tool for any advisor, but it is important to be sure that you are using the right analogy.

Simulation

Through simulation the advisor attempts to create the initial stages of a situation, to get the client to imagine him- or herself in that situation, and then to ask what might happen under the circumstances. The advisor might also play a role in the simulation. On a more sophisticated basis, through the use of computers the advisor might simulate a situation and then introduce variables to determine what the result might be if the client behaved in a particular way. The use of a graphic simulation is a powerful method for getting the client to think about and to understand the consequences of a given course of action. For example, a wealthy man who wants to disinherit a son because of the son's marriage might be asked to imagine the consequences to the son and to the son's relationships with the rest of the family when the son learns that he has been disinherited.

Building Scenarios

A situation may evolve in many different ways, depending on what the participants might do. A technique of trying to ascertain the future is to build scenarios of the various ways in which a situation might unfold and then evaluate the probability of each scenario actually happening. Scenario building might take the form of a dialogue between advisor and client since the client often has important information needed to build the various scenarios and to evaluate their probability. For example, suppose that a frustrated young executive is thinking about quitting her job and therefore seeks your advice. Instead of advising her to leave or to stay, you might instead begin a dialogue with her on the various possible scenarios—if she stayed in the same office, asked for a transfer within the company, quit immediately, or delayed her resignation until she had another job. The client would be asked to examine each scenario carefully to determine the advantages and disadvantages of each one and the likelihood of each coming to pass. Through this process, the client will gain a clear understanding of her options and will probably make her own decision as to what to do, rather than having the advisor recommend a course of action.

Trend projection, analogical forecasting, simulations, and scenario building are four important tools to help the advisor foretell the future. Of course, none is certain. But they do assist the advisor to address the difficulties of helping clients with future action.

4

AGREE
ON
YOUR ROLE

"A consultant is someone who
borrows your watch to tell
you the time, and then keeps the
watch."
—Anonymous, in Szanton, *Not Well Advised*

ADVISORS ARE LIKE ACTORS in a film or musicians in a band:
They have a definite role to play in the advising relationship.
Both advisor and client need to understand and accept that
role for helpful advice to take place. A failure to know your
role as advisor can lead to the same disastrous results as Hamlet
delivering Ophelia's lines or a pianist playing the trumpeter's
part of the score.

All roles have boundaries. As an advisor, you particularly
need to make clear the limits of your role—that is, what you
will and what you will not do for your client. If you will have
to borrow your client's watch to tell him the time, you need
to get agreement on that requirement before you begin. If you
plan to keep the watch, you should make that clear, too.

Defining your role is important for several reasons. First, it determines your strategy for giving advice. It tells you your goal and guides you in focusing your energy, time, and talents in carrying out your task. If your role is to advise the governor of New York on education in state schools, you obviously ought not waste your efforts on suggesting ways to reorganize the department of public works.

Second, a clear definition of the advisor's role gives the client an accurate idea of what the advisor can do to help the client and what the client must contribute to the advising relationship. For example, a counselor who helps high school seniors choose colleges should say at the outset that she will suggest colleges suited to students' ability and interests but that they and their families make the final selection. She should also inform students that they must go through a series of interviews and take a battery of tests in order to provide the information necessary to give helpful advice. An accurate understanding of the advisor's role avoids unrealistic expectations by the client—for instance, that the college advisor has the influence to get students into Harvard despite poor academic records in high school.

Third, an accurate understanding of the advising role allows clients to evaluate the advice they receive. Suppose a management consulting firm has defined its role to include providing emergency advice in crisis situations to client companies. If the partners of the firm make themselves unavailable for long periods of time so that clients cannot quickly get advice when suddenly threatened with a hostile takeover, the consulting firm has clearly failed to fulfill its promised role.

Finally, a clear definition of the advisor's role facilitates the advising process itself by letting clients know what they can and cannot do as the process unfolds. For example, a psychotherapist will make it clear to patients that they are to attend one-hour therapy sessions twice a week, that they should call the therapist in emergencies, but that they may not drop by the therapist's home whenever they want to chat. It is also during the period of role definition that clients gain an understanding of how advisor and client should communicate, what authority the advisor has to act on behalf of the client, and what the client must pay the advisor.

Whether an advisor is a high-priced management consultant to a *Fortune* 500 company or an uncle who wants to help a nephew find a job, the failure to agree upon the advisor's role at the beginning of the relationship can lead to conflict and disappointment between advisor and client later on. A company that hires a management consulting firm on the assumption that the firm will not only design an administrative reorganization but implement it as well may feel seriously misled when the consultant insists that implementation of management reforms is not part of its mission. Similarly, a nephew who expected his uncle to introduce him to potential employers may be bitterly disappointed when he later learns that his uncle is only willing to suggest companies that the nephew should contact. Defining your role at the beginning of your relationship with your client is essential. How, then, should you go about it?

NEGOTIATING YOUR ROLE

Many professional advisors feel that role definition is just a matter of telling clients what they can expect from the advisor. In short, they impose the role they expect to play. Even worse, some professionals such as doctors or lawyers whose professions' traditions are well known to the public assume that clients are already well aware of the roles these professionals play. Consequently, they may not even bother to discuss the roles that they will play in the relationship with patients and clients. Skilled advisors recognize, however, that they can neither assume nor impose their roles. Instead, they know that they must *negotiate* their roles with their clients.

Each client is unique, and each client's problem is distinct. The advisor's role in helping to solve that problem is also special in each case. It is defined by agreement between advisor and client.

Like any process, the process of negotiating your role goes through a series of steps before the parties reach agreement. A first step for the advisor is to determine what role the prospective client sees for the advisor. The advisor often begins this phase simply by asking, "How do you think I can help you?" Ordinarily, the response to this rather simple question will address both the client's problem and what the client thinks the advisor can do about it. So in response to that opening question, the president of a company that has had losses for the last two years may tell a consultant, "I want you to tell me how to restructure our finances." Or a woman who has just discovered that her husband has been having an affair may say to a lawyer, "I want you to tell me how to get a divorce." In effect, the client is offering a role to the advisor.

Often, this phase of the negotiation does not go as smoothly as one might expect. In many cases, the client may be unsure of the exact nature of the problem and have only the vaguest idea of how the advisor can help. Faced with this situation, an advisor must begin a dialogue with the client to learn the dimensions of the client's problem.

Once the client has offered you a role, you can either accept it, reject it, or make a counteroffer. Your response, of course, will depend on your understanding of the nature of the client's problem, your estimation of your ability, and your willingness to help resolve that problem.

A president of a company with declining profits believes that the reason for the company's problems is top management's inability to get the information it needs quickly enough, so she asks you for advice on selecting a new computer system. Rather than agree immediately on that role, you may instead want to determine why management is not getting the information it needs. Upon investigation, you may find that the problem is not the company's computer system, but rather its inefficient organizational structure or the poor training of its employees. So in the process of negotiating your role, you counter the president's offer of a rather narrow role with an offer of broadened responsibility. You sense that the nature of the problem may be different from the president's perception of it.

Similarly, your daughter, who will graduate from college next year, asks your advice on finding a job. Instead of suggesting companies to contact, you tell her that additional courses in accounting and finance will improve her chances on the job market. She resists your attempt to broaden your role and says that she has already decided to take courses next year in history and economics, subjects that she particularly likes. Anyway, accounting is boring. Why can't you just tell her the names of some people to contact for a job?

At this point, you can tell her to find a job on her own or you can agree to limit your role to identifying particular companies, making suggestions about her résumé, and helping her write introductory letters. To persist in urging her to change her academic program will only result in conflict because you are trying to assume an advisory role that she has not agreed to. She wants your advice on jobs, not academics. You can only be an effective advisor if you and your client agree on your role. If you feel strongly that she needs more accounting and finance, you might simply point out that in certain types of jobs additional courses in accounting and finance will give her an advantage, but that in others, a concentration in economics and history will also be valuable.

Advisors sometimes feel insulted or rejected when clients want to limit the advisor's role. They may see the attempt to restrict them as a lack of confidence, a negative judgement by the client on the advisor's ability, knowledge, or even integrity. That reaction is often inaccurate. Clients limit advisors' roles for many reasons. One of the most important is clients' natural desire to stay in control of their own lives. A daughter may reject her father's advice on college courses not because she questions her father's academic judgment but because she feels that shaping her career is her own responsibility.

When advisor and client are unable to agree on an appropriate role, an advisor may have no choice but to decline the offer of advisory relationship. Knowing when to say no to a client can be as important as knowing how to say yes. If, for example, the company CEO insists that a management consultant only make recommendations about new computers instead of examining the company's entire information system, the consultant may decide that such an approach would compromise professional standards and fail in the end to help the client. Moreover, if the advisor does recommend a new computer system but management still does not get the information it needs, the company is likely to blame the consultant for giving bad advice. Faced with this possibility, an advisor might therefore decide to refuse the assignment rather than to undertake an exercise that is not in the client's—and incidentally, the advisor's—best interests.

An advisor's role, once negotiated, is not fixed forever. It can change over time. As mutual confidence grows between advisor and client, the advisor's role may expand. A business satisfied with a consultant's recommendation on new computers may ask for an evaluation of the company's entire information system. A daughter, thinking about a career, may ask her father's advice on courses that will increase chances for a desirable job. In both cases, however, the advisor's role expands not by the advisor's unilateral act, but rather by mutual, often tacit, agreement between the two sides. Consequently, advisors who are tempted to refuse clients because of dissatisfaction with the role they offer should first ask whether it will be possible to expand that role in the future to what they consider appropriate dimensions. A family doctor finds that a hard-driving executive only asks for help when he is ill, but ignores the doctor's advice on exercise, diet, and relaxation. Instead of rejecting the patient or arguing with him constantly over an unhealthy lifestyle, the doctor should try to gain the executive's confidence so that he will come to accept the doctor in the role of a health consultant, rather than just as someone who cures the sick.

THE PROBLEM IS THE PROBLEM

Sometimes a client's problem is so unclear or so complex that an advisor must spend considerable time and energy just to figure out what it is. For example, a community is in turmoil over the beating of a teenage boy by the police. The mayor asks you to advise the town on a better system to supervise police activities. Before you make any recommendation, you need to understand the nature of the relations between community and police—a task that you certainly will not be able to accomplish in a few hours by making a couple of phone calls. In this situation, you should limit your initial role as an advisor to helping define the problem and make that fact clear to your client. You might therefore tell the mayor of the town in conflict: "For now, let me help you figure out just what your problem is. Once we know that, then let's talk about whether and how I can help you solve it."

For any advisor, the process of problem definition is an essential first step—not only for determining the advisor's role but for being of any help at all to the client. In defining the problem, advisors must, of course, rely on their particular professional expertise. A doctor seeking to understand the cause of a pain in a patient's chest must apply medical knowledge. A structural engineer trying to understand why a building is sagging must rely on the science of civil engineering. A management consultant looking for the causes of a factory's declining productivity needs to draw on the fields of organizational behavior, finance, and mechanical engineering. But in addition, all advisors of whatever variety should also bear in mind a few general principles of problem definition as they go about this basic preliminary task.

1. Don't mistake symptoms for the problem. Often clients realize they have a problem only when they experience unpleasant symptoms—heartburn, cracks in the walls, falling profits. Sometimes advisors direct their advice to getting rid of the symptoms rather than correcting the cause of the problem. So a doctor prescribes heartburn medicine for a pain in the chest without bothering to take X rays; a civil engineer recommends plastering the wall, rather than strengthening the foundation; and a management consultant advises firing a few workers to reduce costs, rather than reorganizing the plant.

Defining a problem in terms of its symptoms can set the whole advising process on a path that is not only unlikely to help clients but may actually hurt them in the long run.

2. The client is an important source of information about the problem, so be sure to tap that resource fully. In the rush to define their roles so they can get to work quickly, advisors sometime fail to obtain the client's full knowledge and understanding of the problem. An angry wife tells you about her husband's inattention and prolonged absences from home, and she asks your advice. You tell her to get a divorce lawyer, change the locks on the doors at home, and empty out the joint checking account. Had you discussed the matter with her further, you would have discovered that for her the problem was not ending the marriage but rebuilding her relationship with a husband whose business was threatened with bankruptcy. Overlooking the client as a source of information about the problem can lead to bad advice.

3. Look at the problem from the client's perspective, but not just from the client's perspective. An advisor needs to understand the problem from the client's perspective. That perspective will enable you to learn how the problem affects your clients and what possible solutions will mean for them. At the same time, to examine the problem from only the client's perspective can often lead to incorrect problem definition. For one thing, clients are usually more concerned about symptoms than causes. Consequently, without help they may tend to define the problem in terms of symptoms. For another, your value as an advisor is your particular perspective as a detached, objective observer. That perspective brings to the

task of problem definition elements that the client has over-
looked or deliberately ignored.

DEFINING THE LIMITS OF YOUR ROLE

Once you know the problem, defining your role becomes a
process of negotiation between you and your client. Various
factors will determine the outcome of that negotiation. As
an advisor, you need to understand these factors in order to
negotiate your role.

1. Your resources. Your resources, both intellectual and physical, will affect your role in the advising relationship. Once
you understand the problem, you have to ask yourself a first
and fundamental question: Do I have the knowledge, skills,
and time to help my client? An honest answer to that question
may lead you to decline the role of advisor completely. For
example, in examining the problem between a community
and its police force, you may conclude that you simply do not
know enough about social problems of this kind to be of any
help or that studying the nature of the problem would require
a staff of researchers far larger than what your organization
now employs. On the other hand, you may feel you have only
enough resources to give a client limited help. You may be
able to help a town in conflict understand the causes of conflict
between the community and the police, but you may not have
the expertise in police procedures to recommend a specific
system for police supervision. You may be able to advise your
son on strategies to find a job, but you may not know specific
corporate executives that he should ask for interviews. Your
resources, then, are important factors determining the role
you can play.

2. *Your client's resources.* Your client's resources—both tangible and intangible—will also affect the role you play. At the most basic level, whether your client has the money to pay your fee will determine what, if anything, you can do for him. Sometimes management consultants, in negotiating a role with their clients, propose two different "scopes of work" having different price tags—a broad scope with a large cost and a narrow scope with a reduced one.

But money is not your client's only resource. The client's knowledge and experience will also influence the limits of your role. A financial advisor to an experienced corporate executive may have a different, perhaps more limited role in advising on investments than she would have in counseling a widow without any business experience. Similarly, a political consultant to a young lawyer running for election for the first time to the House of Representatives would probably play a different role than if she were advising a senior congressman running for reelection for the tenth time. The senior congressman, because of his experience in past elections, brings significant resources to the political campaign and therefore would probably give the consultant a different, possibly more narrow role than would the candidate running for the first time.

3. *Trust and confidence between client and advisor.* The strength of the feeling of trust and confidence between advisor and client also affects the limits of the advisor's role. Obviously, the more confidence that a client has in an advisor, the more likely that the advisor will have a broad role in the advising relationship. A constant challenge of any advisor is to gain the trust of clients and then to preserve it over the life of their relationship.

The strength of trust that clients have in an advisor will

depend on many things. Certainly, the resources and reputation that the advisor brings to the task have a major influence in establishing confidence. For example, a multinational firm seeking advice on financing a new factory is likely to have more confidence in a famous Wall Street investment bank than in an associate professor of finance at a midwestern university.

But perhaps more important than resources and reputation is the nature of the experience that the client has already had with the advisor. If that experience has been positive and productive, the client is likely to have confidence in the advisor and therefore allow a broad role. Without that experience, clients generally want to restrict their advisors' role until they have proven themselves. If the ten-term congressman has had the same political advisor throughout many successful campaigns, he will probably give the consultant a broad role and rely heavily on her advice in devising campaign strategy, selecting political advertisements, and hiring staff. On the other hand, the young lawyer making her first run for Congress may rely much less on the advice of a consultant with whom she has had no experience.

4. Law and ethics. The law and the ethics of your particular profession will also influence your role as an advisor. For example, the law requires a doctor to obtain the "informed consent" of a patient before operating, giving an injection, or administering medication. It also prohibits an attorney from using business information learned from a client for the attorney's personal profit. So the law sets down limits on what the advisor can and cannot do in relationships with clients. Numerous professions, from lawyers and doctors to accountants and engineers, also have codes of ethics to guide their members in serving clients. These codes are invariably concerned with setting certain limits on the roles played by their members in advising clients.

YOUR NEGOTIATED ROLE

The result of negotiation over your role may be an elaborate contract, like those used by management consultants, or simply a tacit understanding, as when an uncle agrees to advise a nephew on a career. But whatever role you agree upon with your client, you must recognize that in the end the problem is your client's, not yours.

The definition of boundaries protects not only clients but also advisors. The temptation is strong for any conscientious advisor to take ownership of the client's problem and to identify with the client's situation—to inevitably and gradually assume the client's role. While an advisor's empathy with a client is essential for effective counseling, it is equally essential to maintain the distinct roles of advisor and client. It is easy, for example, for a father advising a son on finding a job to see the job search as the father's problem, not the son's. It is also easy for a lawyer representing a teenager unjustly accused of murder to make freeing the client a personal cause.

Commitment to a client always holds the risk that the advisor will assume some or all of the client's role, a phenomenon that can obstruct effective advising. First, it can cause the advisor to lose objectivity and independent perspective, the very things that the client wanted in seeking out an advisor. Second, it can lead to actions by the advisor that disempower the client, that infringe on the client's rights as an independent person. For example, a father may become so anxious about a son's job prospects that he coerces the son to make certain career decisions—or, worse—tries to make those decisions for his son. He might therefore send his son's résumé to companies without the son's permission or make appointments for job interviews without consulting him.

All advisors, whether fathers or gurus, need to remember that they are not puppet masters and that their clients are not puppets. Advising, as we shall see in the next chapter, is by its very nature a collaborative activity, a partnership between advisor and client.

5

NEVER GIVE
A SOLO
PERFORMANCE

"The first condition of a good Counsellour
is that his Ends, and Interest, be not
inconsistent with the Ends and Interest of
him he Counselleth."
—Hobbes, *Leviathan*

SOME ADVISORS THINK THEY ARE HIRED GUNS. Others think they
are the Lone Ranger. In either case, they like to project the
image of individualist heros who arrive on the scene and work
alone to rescue clients from their troubles. So lawyers see
themselves as champions of their clients in the search for
justice, and doctors do battle for their patients in the fight
against disease. Even management consultants like to think
that they can single-handedly turn around a troubled company. The client in these scenarios is just an object for the
advisor's heroic efforts, an object that contributes little or
nothing to solving the problem. Even worse, for some advisors
the client is merely a necessary nuisance who pays the bills.
If the client will just cooperate, stay out of the way, and follow
orders, the advisor will see to it that the client's problem is

solved. For these kinds of advisors, advising—if it *is* an art—is best done as a solo performance or a one-person show.

PLAY AT LEAST A DUET

Effective advising is always a duet, at the very least. A truly artful advisor never gives a solo performance and never presents a one-person show. On the contrary, skilled advising requires the active participation of the client. One of the great challenges for any advisor is to secure from the client a maximum contribution to the advising process.

For many advisors, the idea that the client has something other than fees to contribute to advising is difficult to accept. After all, the very reason that the client has sought the service of an advisor is because the advisor has superior knowledge—knowledge that the client lacks. For all advisors, the professional schools they attended and the cultures of the professions to which they belong emphasize repeatedly in many ways that specialized knowledge is their primary asset. It is what distinguishes them from the rest of humanity, a group they generally and sometimes condescendingly refer to as "laymen."

From the diplomas they hang on their walls to the letters that they place after their names, advisors throughout their professional lives continually emphasize in both subtle and direct ways that they have expertise that others lack. As a result, advisors in all professions believe that clients do not have the knowledge to solve their problems, but that advisors do. So what can clients possibly contribute to solving the problem, except uninformed and unenlightened opinions that in the end will only complicate and delay finding a solution? Moreover, clients become emotionally wrapped up in their problems and fail to see their long-term interests. The advisor brings objectivity, perspective, and vision.

The fact that an advisor has specialized knowledge about a client's problem does not mean that the client has nothing to contribute to solving it. In reality, the client, whether a basketball player seeking advice about pains in his knees or a company wanting counsel about declining profits, has indispensable information to give to the advising process. Usually, the more that advisors view a problem as technical—one requiring specialized knowledge—the less importance they give to the client's participation in the advising process. In point of fact, of course, few problems—perhaps none—are purely technical in nature. Whether the goal is reorganizing a government department or choosing the best computer system for an office, whether the challenge is to recommend a sound estate plan for an aging couple or the right strategy for a machine tool company to enter the Asian market, the wise solution to the problem must account for many factors that are not purely scientific or technical—factors that involve the knowledge, values, and desires of the client.

Most problems have both a technical and a nontechnical dimension. While the advisor may be the primary—or, indeed, the only—source of knowledge on the technical dimensions, the client usually knows far more about the nontechnical aspects. An advisor who fails to obtain this knowledge from the client is in effect making recommendations and giving advice on incomplete information. For example, a financial planner must understand the couple's lifestyle and goals to make an estate plan, and a business consultant must learn about the machine tool company's existing business and capabilities to advise on a strategy for Asia.

In the mid-1970s, Egypt was experiencing significant financial problems and its government was incurring large budget deficits. The government therefore asked the International

Monetary Fund for help. After reviewing the situation, IMF officials strongly advised Egypt to eliminate the subsidies it was granting on such basic foodstuffs as flour and cooking oil as the best way to reduce the country's chronic budgetary deficits. Ending the subsidies would put Egypt's public finances on a sound basis at long last.

From the technical economic point of view, the IMF's advice was correct. But Egypt's problems were not purely economic; they had significant political dimensions as well. Egypt needed subsidies to maintain social peace in a country where a large part of the population suffered from great poverty. The IMF advisors failed to listen to government officials in making their recommendations; consequently, they virtually ignored the political implications of suddenly eliminating food subsidies for a population that had relied on low food prices for many years. The IMF economists saw the problem as exclusively economic and felt no need to encourage government officials to participate in shaping the IMF recommendations. After all, the bad economics of the government had caused the budget deficit problem in the first place, so what could that same government possibly contribute to a solution?

When the Egyptian government, under pressure from the IMF, finally did cut the subsidies, food prices rose sharply and riots broke out in Egypt's cities. Damage was great and a police crackdown failed to end the disturbances. Finally, in order to bring peace to the country, the government had to restore subsidies. Egyptian officials may have been less expert than IMF economists on the economic impact of subsidies, but they were clearly experts on the political situation in their own country—a situation that the IMF foreign advisors failed to comprehend fully. It is essential, then, for an advisor to involve the client in the advising process because the client is an important—and sometimes the only—source of information upon which to base good advice in the particular case at hand.

A second reason that you should involve the client in the advising process is that the problem you are trying to solve is the client's, not yours. It is the client, not you, who must make the decision on an appropriate course of action. It is the client, not you, who must order and pay for the new computer system, implement the recommended administrative organization, accept the proposed estate plan, and follow the right strategy to enter a new market. And it is the client, not you, who must bear the consequences of these decisions. Clients make these choices not only on technical grounds but also on the basis of their own values, goals, and desires. The advisor's job is not to give the client the "right" answer, but rather to present a range of options from which the client can make a final choice. As one experienced Wall Street lawyer said, "When I first started practicing law, I thought my job was to give the client the answer to his problem. Now, after thirty years of practice, I know that my job is to help my client discover the answer for himself."

WORK ON THE RELATIONSHIP

The wise advisor respects the client's right to decide on the appropriate course of action. Indeed, from the moment that you agree to be an advisor you should make it clear to your clients that they are the primary decision makers and that therefore they must participate with you in shaping the advice that you will offer to solve their problems. You need to stress that advising is above all a *working relationship* between advisor and client. No working relationship can be run productively by one person. Just as you can't play a solo tennis match or a solo game of catch, you can't effectively advise clients without their active participation in the advising process.

A final reason to avoid solo performances is that your clients are more likely to follow advice if they have played a role in shaping it than if they have been totally isolated from the process. Clients not only want the right answer, they want an answer that meets their particular values, goals, and aspirations. If they have participated in finding that answer, they usually feel more secure that it meets their values than if they had nothing to do with making the decision. Moreover, by participating, they will often gain a better understanding of the proposed solution than if it is presented to them all at once as a finished product.

This principle was clearly illustrated a few years ago when a small electronics company that had recently made a public offering of its shares hired a consultant to advise on a new format and cover for its annual report. After receiving the assignment in a lengthy meeting with the company's president, the design consultant retreated to his studio to work. Four weeks later, with the aid of a video and large mock-ups of the cover, the consultant presented a revolutionary new design with great drama and flare. At first the executives of the client company found the designs stunning, but with time they began to have doubts. How would shareholders react to the new design? Even though it was beautiful, did the new design really reflect the company's mission and values? Indeed, did the consulting designer really understand those values? How could he, since he had spent so little time with the company? In the end, the company decided to reject the new design.

The following year the company, still dissatisfied with its annual report, hired another advisor to propose a new format.

This designer spent much time at the company and talked to a wide range of staff, from the president to the factory foreman. As she developed design ideas, she would test them out on various company executives to get their reaction. When she completed her work and presented the final design, the company's executive team immediately accepted it. The design was strong and attractive. But the primary reasons for its acceptance were first, that the client felt that the designer really knew the company, and second, that the design process involved extensive client participation and thus embodied important ideas about the company.

A neutral outside observer comparing both designs would have found each to be attractive and acceptable. The participation by the client in the development of one and not the other led the company management, however, to see vast and important differences between the two.

What this incident clearly demonstrates is that the relationship between advisor and client can affect the quality and acceptability of the advice. In short, advice cannot be evaluated in isolation from the advising relationship that produced it. In the first case, the designer failed to establish a good working relationship with the client company; in the second case, the designer was clearly more successful because of the productive relationship that she managed to create with the company's executives. Similarly, a student seeking advice on an academic program may receive the exact same advice from two professors. Both advise him to take calculus—a subject that scares him. The first time he hears this advice, it comes from the professor whom he hardly knows, so he rejects it. The second time the advice comes from the professor with whom he has worked closely in the past and whom he trusts. As a result of advice from the second professor, the student signs up for calculus. It was the nature of the relationship between student and professor, rather than the nature of the advice itself, that caused him to reject the first advice but accept the second.

The lesson of these cases is that the artful advisor must be at least as concerned about developing an effective working relationship with a client as in shaping the advice that will ultimately be offered. Advisors who forget this rule and attempt to give a solo performance usually find that the advice they offer is not readily accepted or understood. Thus the effective advisor should always remember this fundamental principle: *Work on the relationship with your client just as much as you work on the advice you give.* For the skillful advisor, results are in the relationship.

Advisors who consider the scientific or technical correctness of their advice to be their primary goal may be tempted to dismiss the importance of a good working relationship as mere politics or bedside manner. The point of this chapter is that a good working relationship between advisor and client is essential to giving good advice. It enables you to gain the information you need and it strengthens the client's confidence. Failure to pay attention to the relationship between advisor and client can reduce the quality of the advice that is ultimately offered. So the relationship is not a superficial part of the advising process; rather, it goes to its very essence.

If the relationship between advisor and client is so important, precisely what kind of relationship should exist? What are the characteristics of a good working relationship? The answers to these questions are vital. Without a strong understanding of the important elements of this relationship, how can an advisor and client hope to create one?

FOUR BUILDING BLOCKS OF A WORKING RELATIONSHIP

A good working relationship rests on four building blocks:

Communication
Commitment
Reliability
Respect

1. **Communication.** A good working relationship between advisor and client is, first of all, a two-way *communication*, a relationship where information flows easily in *both* directions. Effective communication means that the advisor must be as prepared to listen to a client as to talk to him or her. Indeed, they each must be ready to talk to and to listen to each other. For the advisor, communication is more than delivering advice. It is important to keep the client informed about the process as it unfolds.

According to surveys taken in several professions, a primary cause of clients' dissatisfaction is the advisors' failure to keep them adequately informed about what they were doing and what they intended to do. Even though an advisor may be working hard on a problem, a client may feel neglected or even abandoned unless he or she hears from the advisor about the progress being made. Thus the effective advisor, rather than to deliver advice all at once with great fanfare, will communicate regularly with the client to keep him or her informed about developments. At the same time, the experienced advisor will listen patiently and encouragingly to what the client has to say. It is well to remember that clients often find that the best advising sessions are those where they have had a good chance to talk.

2. **Commitment.** A good working relationship is one in which advisors clearly convey to clients that they are working to help them. It is also one in which the client believes that, in the words of Thomas Hobbes, the advisor's "Ends, and Interest, be not inconsistent" with the client's. In short, *commitment* of the advisor to the client is another basic foundation of a good working relationship. Commitment, however, is more than a mere declaration by the advisor to the client that "I am on your side." The client will judge whether the advisor has a genuine commitment on the basis of the advisor's behavior over the course of the relationship. In particular, the client will be watching to see whether the advisor really cares about the client and is intent on making a genuine effort to help solve the client's problem.

3. **Reliability.** A third element in a good working relationship is *reliability*. A client, as its Latin origin indicates, is a person who has someone to lean on. So a client needs a reliable support. Just as leaning on an unreliable crutch can prove disastrous for an accident victim, leaning on an unreliable advisor can often cause clients more damage than if they had never decided to engage an advisor in the first place. For example, an elderly widow who lets her savings be invested by an unreliable financial consultant may in the end be worse off than if she had left her money in a savings bank.

Reliability has many dimensions. It means that the advisor's conduct should be predictable. Thus the advice given should seem to the client to respond to the problem that the advisor and client have identified. A company that hires a consultant to provide a marketing strategy will consider him unreliable if he puts aside this assignment and instead begins writing memoranda to the company president on the firm's need for a new teleconferencing system.

Reliability also means that the advisor should keep his promises and commitments to the client. A management consultant who consistently submits reports to the client two months late, a lawyer who persistently fails to appear for appointments, or the consulting engineer who never returns a client's telephone calls will soon be seen as unreliable. Once a client feels that an advisor is unreliable, that judgment will inevitably become an obstacle to developing a good working relationship.

Reliability also implies honesty. The client expects and demands honesty from the advisor. One of the quickest ways to erode a good working relationship is for an advisor to say or do something that seems dishonest. Once the client suspects that the advisor is acting in his own ends and interests rather than in those of the client, the relationship is at an end.

4. Respect. A final but no less important building block for a good working relationship is *respect*—respect for the client as a person. Many advisors' basic approach to clients is to show how much the advisors know. They believe that by demonstrating their superior knowledge they will command the respect and loyalty of their clients. But respect, like communication, is a two-way process. Too often the way advisors show their superior knowledge is by belittling the knowledge of their clients and constantly pointing out their clients' ignorance. To say to your client, as one lawyer often did to his, "Let me do the thinking for both of us," is hardly a statement of respect for the client's intelligence.

A productive working relationship cannot develop if an advisor is constantly sending messages in both word and deed that the client is ignorant. It is important to remember that no matter how many academic degrees you may have and no matter how high your status in your profession, your clients are generally knowledgeable in their own areas of activity. You also need to remember that the purpose of your words and actions is to advance your clients' interests, not your own ego. Clients prefer advisors who do not try to impress them constantly, who avoid technical jargon, and who do not act condescendingly. In short, they want advisors who treat them with respect.

Thus there are four foundation stones to building a good working relationship: communication, commitment, reliability, and respect. Even with knowledge of each of these four foundation stones, the artful advisor faces a challenge in building and maintaining a good relationship with the client.

GETTING YOUR CLIENT TO PLAY

Clients do not always participate energetically in the advising process. Sometimes they refuse to participate at all. What should you do if your client wants you to give a solo performance? What should you do to get your clients to play a duet with you? How should an advisor deal with this kind of reluctant client? Here are a few ways to get your client to play:

1. You should make it clear from the very beginning of the relationship that your client, for all the reasons stated above, needs to participate in the advising process.

2. You should seek to understand the reasons why your client is reluctant to participate. For some clients, their experience with autocratic advisors in the past may have taught them their place—subservience to the perceived superior status and wisdom of their advisors. Others may fear that participation in the process may lead to unpleasant results or that they will have to take responsibility for difficult decisions that they would prefer to avoid. For example, one aging executive refused to allow his doctor to weigh him during annual physical examinations in hopes of avoiding discussions of his need to lose weight. Similarly, the management of an ailing subsidiary may refuse to cooperate with a consultant sent by the parent company in order to undermine the consultant's report, which they fear will lead to reductions in staff.

3. Once you understand the cause of client reluctance, you need to devise a strategy to cope with it. For example, it may be better not to insist on weighing the patient if that will facilitate a better relationship between doctor and patient. Similarly, a management consultant, faced with an uncooperative subsidiary, might seek to find other sources for the needed information or find ways to assure the subsidiary's executives that they will have a full opportunity to review the consultant's report before it is submitted to the parent company.

4. You should be patient in dealing with a reluctant client. In the early stages of the relationship, clients evaluate their advisors. They judge their commitment, reliability, and competence, and they may withhold active participation until they feel that their advisors are persons they can rely on.

5. You should be sure that you know your clients and you should allow your clients to know you. Apply the principles outlined in chapter 2 to gain this knowledge.

6. As a skilled advisor, you should be a genuine consultant. That is, you should actively consult your clients throughout the advising process to determine their views and feelings about their problem. The design consultant in the case cited earlier drew her effectiveness not only from her artistic talents but also from the way that she actively consulted the client throughout the development of the design for the company's new annual report.

This chapter has stressed the importance of the relationship between advisor and client to the art of advice. Without a good working relationship, good advising is virtually impossible. But a relationship itself is not advice. It is advice that we must look at next.

6

MAKE THE
PROCESS CLEAR
AND CONSTRUCTIVE

"Anything that is good in itself
must be capable of being expressed
clearly and precisely. The moment I
come across words that are not very
clear . . . I am left with the conclusion
that they are either *mistaken* or *deceitful*."
—Metternich, in De Sauvigny,
Metternich and His Times

THE MEDIUM IS THE PROCESS

EVERY ARTIST WORKS IN A PARTICULAR MEDIUM. Painters work
in oils or watercolors. Sculptors toil in stone or clay. Ballerinas
express themselves in the movements of the dance. For an
advisor, the medium is the process—the *way* of giving advice.
Just as painters, sculptors, and dancers have to think hard and
systematically about their medium to master their art, skilled
advisors must pay attention to the advising process to help
their clients.

PAY ATTENTION TO THE PROCESS

Advising is a process—a consciously guided, progressive movement toward a desired goal. The goal is to help the client solve a problem. To be effective, advisors must master the process of giving advice, as well as the substance of the advice that they deliver to the client. Too often, advisors see their job exclusively as finding the right information to solve the client's problem. They concentrate on recommending the right drug to improve a patient's health, the exact formula to reduce a university's deficit, or the precise technology to increase a factory's productivity. As a result, they fail to think about the process that will allow them to develop and deliver the best solution to the client's problems.

Skillful advisors, on the other hand, know that they must give considerable thought to constructing and managing a process that will create and deliver the kind of advice that a particular client needs. The process for creating and delivering advice to a large state university will differ from that used to help a small denominational college. The process for advising a young man coping with AIDS will not be the same as the process for counseling an elderly woman who is overweight. The specific nature of the advising process will also depend on the factors discussed in previous chapters—on the advisor's knowledge of the client (chapter 2), on the role given the advisor (chapter 4), and on the relationship between advisor and client (chapter 5).

THE STEPS OF THE PROCESS

Like any process, advising passes through a series of distinct steps. If advisor and client are to work effectively together, both must understand these steps. Not only will that understanding help the advisor manage the process, it will also allow the client to make a greater contribution to the search for solutions than if the process were to remain a mystery. For example, if the executives of an ailing company know at the outset how a management consultant intends to develop recommendations to improve profitability, they will understand the amount of time and resources that the company will have to commit to the process. That understanding may prevent unrealistic expectations, for example, that the management consultant will deliver a magic solution that will completely cure the company's troubles within a month. Disappointed expectations can harm an advising relationship.

The advising process consists of seven fairly distinct steps.

1. Get to know your client. As chapter 2 points out, a first and essential task for any advisor is to get to know the client. You really cannot be helpful unless you know the person you are trying to help. You therefore need to refer to the principles and techniques discussed in that chapter.

2. Define the problem. The second step in the advising process seeks to define the client's problem. To understand the client's problem, you must look at it—at least initially—from the client's point of view. What is it that concerns the client? What is the client really bothered about? Seeing the problem from the client's point of view does not mean that you must accept the client's explanation of it. A middle-level executive who has twenty years' experience with a corporation seeks your advice because he feels that he is the victim of age discrimination. He thinks that management has judged him to be too old to be effective. The basic problem for the client is not age discrimination, but rather his inability to advance in the company—to receive promotions and pay raises. The cause of the problem may indeed be age discrimination, but it could also be something else—poor job performance, losses by the company, or lack of growth in the industry. So at the outset of defining the problem with the client, the advisor needs to make a distinction between the nature of the problem and the nature of its causes. To define the problem accurately, both advisor and client must seek the objective facts and resist the impulse to label the problem prematurely. For example, a lawyer who is consulted by an aggrieved wife should avoid seeing the problem as a divorce case, but rather as a problem of a wife whose relations with her husband are troubled. Of course, once the advisor has an understanding of the problem both advisor and client must seek its causes and consequences in order to define it completely.

3. Determine your client's objectives. The third phase of the advising process seeks to determine the client's objectives. What is it that the client wants? Does the twenty-year manager really want to stay with the corporation with a slightly better paying job and a more impressive title? Or does he want to do something else with his life? The answer to these questions, of course, will determine whether the advisor helps the manager overcome obstacles to promotion within the organization or instead devises a strategy for the client to leave the company gracefully with a substantial severance payment and set up his own business. Similarly, does the troubled wife want to end the marriage or does she want to find a way to rebuild her relationship with her husband? Or does she want to take some time to think about her situation? A determination of client objectives is crucial. If you don't define your client's objectives correctly, the rest of the advising process will fail.

Sometimes advisors either consciously or unconsciously try to determine objectives for the client. A college professor might push a talented student toward a career in architecture because the professor sees the student as a young Frank Lloyd Wright. Or a financial advisor, looking forward eagerly to retirement in Florida, assumes that a client plans to retire at sixty-five when, in fact, she really wants to start a new career as a consultant. Objectives are the client's, not the advisor's. The skilled advisor takes care to avoid imposing objectives during the advising process.

Sometimes a client, unsure of what goals to pursue, asks the advisor what to do. In this situation, the advisor should begin a dialogue to define those objectives based on the client's own feelings and values rather than tell a client what objectives to pursue. So instead of recommending that the manager quit his job or sue his employer, have a long talk with him to learn about his goals and aspirations in life and his feelings and beliefs about the company.

4. Identify the options. In the fourth phase of the process, advisor and client try to identify possible options that will allow the client to achieve the desired objective. The cancer patient, whose objective is to regain good health, would review various types of available treatments—chemotherapy, surgery, radiation. Or the failing company, trying to return to profitability, would examine possible options, such as laying off workers, strengthening marketing operations, investing in new equipment, or finding a merger partner.

The goal in this phase is to develop as many options as possible. It is here that advisor and client need to be at their most creative. Rather than evaluate an option as it is presented, advisor and client should first try to determine a whole range of possible options without deciding whether any of them is good or bad. In their dialogue during this phase, advisor and client should avoid words and actions that might stifle creative option making. For example, an executive hesitantly suggests to the management consultant that the company could strengthen its sales force to improve profits. The consultant immediately responds: "I have seen that tried before and it doesn't work without dealing with the basic problem that your technology is too old." That abrupt response may indeed be correct, but it is not likely to encourage other managers to offer suggestions. Rather, the skillful advisor, conscious of the importance of the process, would have responded: "That is one option that we will need to look at."

Many useful ideas will come from your clients, and you therefore need to think constantly about ways of encouraging them to offer as many creative options as possible. Some clients are eager to make suggestions. Others are more hesitant. After all, that is why they hired you. The inexperienced advisor is sometimes reluctant to seek clients' ideas for fear that they will believe the advisor is uninformed. The judicious phrasing of questions can avoid this result. For example, an advisor seeking ideas might ask the client: "What have you already tried? What options have you thought about trying?" The thrust of this approach is to appear to ask for background information rather than for suggestions on substantive solutions.

A second and equally important reason exists for obtaining the client's participation in identifying options. Clients are likely to be more committed to carrying out their own ideas than those advanced by the advisor alone. Clients who recognize a proposed solution as their own will ordinarily devote increased effort and resources to making it work.

A doctor who had been unsuccessfully advising patients to stop smoking adopted another approach. He began to ask them: "What would it take to get you to stop smoking?" In effect, the doctor, as medical advisor, was asking his patients to suggest options to deal with their smoking problem. The result of this change in tactics had three consequences. First, it prompted patients to think seriously about their problem, rather than to concentrate on fending off the doctor's unwelcome advice. Second, it often generated options which the doctor and patient could develop into a plan to stop smoking. And third, patients undertook these no-smoking programs with a sense of commitment since they viewed these programs as their own, not the doctor's.

Advisors should try to use this approach in other situations where the objective is clear but the client is unable or unwilling to take steps to achieve it. Rather than trying to overpower the client with good advice, the advisor should seek a dialogue about possible options. For example, a counselor might ask a student in academic difficulties: "What will it take to get you to give more time and attention to your studies?" Or an economic advisor to a developing country might ask the finance minister: "What measures would be necessary to allow the government to reduce subsidies to state-owned industries?" While this kind of question may seem a meek way of giving advice, it can be a powerful stimulus to client action—sometimes more powerful than a direct recommendation.

5. Evaluate the options. Having identified possible options, the advisor and client next need to evaluate them to determine their costs, their benefits, their consequences, and their likelihood of allowing the client to achieve the desired objectives.

It is here that the advisor's experience and technical knowledge are particularly important. Through the application of that knowledge to each option, the advisor can determine the option's impact on the client's situation—what will work and what won't, what each will cost, and what results can be expected.

Through evaluation, the advisor has the power to influence the client's final decision. Consequently, advisors should not mislead themselves or their clients into believing that they have nothing to do with the final decision. An advisor can use this evaluative power for the good of the client or for dubious purposes. Unscrupulous advisors who want to influence a decision in a particular way often do so at this stage of the advising process. For example, an investment advisor who wants a client to invest in a particular biotechnology company in which the advisor has an interest will influence the client by emphasizing the advantages of that stock when compared with other investment options.

On the other hand, the knowledge gained in the evaluation phase can help a client make the right decision. In one case, the children of a dying man in a hospital were divided as to whether to keep him alive at all costs or to enter a Do Not Resuscitate (DNR) order to prevent the use of artificial life-support systems. The attending physician felt that a DNR order should be entered, but she made no recommendation to the family. Finally, at their request, she gave a detailed description of the patient's likely condition should acute infection reoccur and he were to be placed on life-support systems. That description so distressed the family members that they agreed not to keep their father alive by artificial means. The doctor's evaluation of the options clearly influenced the family's decision.

6. Your client decides on a course of action. Ultimately, in the advising process, the client must make a decision to adopt a definite course of action or to do nothing. The decision is the client's, but the advisor can legitimately play a role in at least three situations.

First, faced with several options, all of which the advisor has carefully evaluated, the client may turn to the advisor and ask: "What would you do?" For example, at the hospital in the case discussed earlier, instead of seeking more information the family members of a dying relative might have asked the doctor for a definite recommendation on whether to enter a Do Not Resuscitate order. Should advisors tell their clients what to do? If your client asks what you would do, you should answer. But you should base your response on your client's values and situation. If the problem is one of values—whether to keep a patient alive at all or let him die peacefully—you should make your values known to the client when you answer the question, What would you do?

A second situation in which an advisor should actively seek to influence the client's decision is where the client is about to make an immoral or illegal decision. For example, as a management consultant to a failing company seeking to find ways to improve profitability you should use your influence to prevent the company from making a decision that would lower costs by polluting the environment.

And finally, a third case in which an advisor may legitimately seek to intervene in a client's decision is when the client has clearly misjudged the likely outcome of a particular course of action. For example, if a patient with syphilis decides to do nothing because he is convinced his condition will clear up with time, a doctor should actively seek to change the patient's decision to forgo treatment. Similarly, if a failing student decides not to study for examinations because she believes they are just a matter of luck, a faculty advisor would be justified in trying to persuade the student that she has chosen an approach that will only lead to disaster.

7. Assess the results. A final phase in the advising process should take place when client and advisor assess the results of the client's decision. Unfortunately, this phase fails to occur in many advising relationships. If the decision has brought satisfactory results, the client may feel no need to tell the advisor. For example, a company that has paid for a management consultant's report will implement it and, if it works, forget to tell the consultant what happened. A college senior who asked for career advice from an experienced manager may feel too embarrassed to tell the advisor that he still has not found a job six months later.

Nonetheless, in developing an appropriate process for the client, the skilled advisor should always seek to program a final phase where the two can review and evaluate the results of the client's decision. Often actions taken on one decision only lead to the necessity of making other related decisions; assessment of the results of that first decision can help the client in making those subsequent decisions. For example, the college senior may have secured a job thanks to the advice of the manager but now needs help on shaping strategy for career development with his new employer.

Assessment is also important to educate the advisor. It will inform the advisor about the soundness of particular advice in a specific situation—what works and what doesn't—and it will also give the advisor further information about the client. That information will help the advisor increase effectiveness the next time that the client seeks help.

For these reasons, you should tell your clients that you want to know the results of their decisions and offer to meet with them to keep abreast of developments. If clients fail to report back, you may want to take the initiative in asking them what happened as a result of your advice.

The seven steps in the advising process are summarized in the accompanying diagram. The amount of time and resources that advisor and client devote to any particular phase will depend on the client's situation, the advisor's experience, and the nature of the problem to be solved. In practice, advising is never as straightforward as this diagram would suggest. Nevertheless, an understanding of the advising phases will help advisor and client construct a process to meet the client's needs.

ADVISING IS TEACHING

As you move through each step in the advising process, you need to remember that advising is teaching. It is individualized instruction tailored to the life, needs, and objectives of the client. An effective advisor is, above all, a good teacher, and good teaching is both clear and constructive.

The ultimate test of good teaching is not whether the professor has delivered a brilliant lecture, but whether the students have actually learned something. So too the basic test of good advising is not whether the advisor has presented a technically perfect opinion, but whether the client is actually better able to deal with a problem. For this kind of help to take place, the advisor's ability to communicate effectively with the client is essential.

Effective communication is fundamental to the art of advice. Just as artists are judged by their ability to move their

SEVEN STEPS IN THE ADVISING PROCESS

1. Get to Know Your Client

↓

2. Define the Problem

↓

3. Determine Your Client's Objectives

↓

4. Identify the Options

↓

5. Evaluate the Options

↓

6. Your Client Decides on a Course of Action

↓

7. Assess the Results

audiences, advisors should be measured by their ability to teach and to communicate with their clients. Physicians, regardless of their number of years of specialized training, cannot be good advisors if their patients do not clearly understand them. Lawyers, regardless of their standing in the profession, fail as counselors when their clients cannot comprehend their advice. Yet we often assume that doctors, lawyers, and other professionals are skilled advisors just because they command vast technical knowledge and are able to restate it when asked. That assumption is like declaring an actor or singer, whose words are indistinct for theater audiences beyond the fifth row, to be great artists just because they have had years of training at the Royal Shakespeare Company or the Juilliard School. The test of effective advising resides in the mind of the recipient, not in the imagination of the sender.

MAKE IT CLEAR

Effective communication requires clarity, and clarity demands effort. Although the clear tones of an opera singer seem to resonate easily throughout the hall at La Scala, they are the product of years of training and practice. While the colors in a Monet painting may appear as natural as sunlight itself, they are the result of a lifetime of work. So too advisors can only give clarity to their advice through thought, concentration, and effort.

An advisor's first rule of clarity is to be sensitive to clients throughout the advising process. You must be aware of whether your clients understand what you are communicating.

To communicate effectively, skillful advisors must constantly and simultaneously be aware of three things: (1) their own words and actions, (2) the meaning that their clients give to those words and actions, and (3) the words and actions of their clients. As a result, a good advisor is like a director in a television studio watching three TV monitors showing the images taken by three different cameras of the same set. Each monitor displays a different angle, or dimension, of the same

THE ADVISOR'S THREE CAMERAS

CAMERA NO. 1:
FOCUS ON YOUR CLIENT'S WORDS AND ACTIONS

CAMERA NO. 2:
FOCUS ON YOUR WORDS AND ACTIONS

CAMERA NO. 3:
FOCUS ON THE EFFECT OF YOUR WORDS AND ACTIONS ON YOUR CLIENT

activity. Like the television director, an advisor must constantly process information from each monitor and then make decisions about next steps.

An advisor must also understand the communication process—particularly the various phases of that process. Problems and complications can arise at each phase to obstruct clarity in communication between advisor and client. Let's look at these phases.

Transmission

The communication process begins with the *transmission* of a message by the advisor to the client. For example, the physician may say to a client, "You need tests." Or a political consultant may tell a Senate candidate, "You have to avoid taking a position on free trade." Unfortunately, for many advisors who see themselves as oracles, the communication process stops here. In fact, transmission is only the beginning.

Perception

Transmission of information by the advisor is followed by the client's *perception* of the statement. Did a nervous patient with chest pains actually hear the words "You need tests"? Or did his emotions make him hear something else—for example, "You need rest"? Did the busy candidate rushing from one campaign event to another actually hear his consultant advise against taking a position on free trade or were those words blocked out by the commotion in campaign headquarters or the need to focus attention on the next speech? Thus every advisor delivering advice must make sure that the client perceived it. Often the surrounding environment or the state of mind of the client can interfere with the perception. Consequently, the advisor should seek to minimize the factors that obstruct perception—worry, surrounding noise, ongoing activity. Unless accurate perception takes place, communication between advisor and client will fail.

To assure perception of the message, an artful advisor will plan the circumstances and means of delivering the message. For example, a campaign advisor would probably try to deliver his message about free trade when the candidate is alone rather than when he is surrounded by his staff seeking his signature on letters and reports. A doctor would want to discuss the need for tests in the quiet of her office and without the interruption of telephone calls and other patients.

For many advisors, the ability to orchestrate the circumstances for delivery of the message depends on access to the client. Some advisors, like doctors treating an invalid, have almost unrestricted access to the client. Others, like policy advisors to presidents, may have only limited access and therefore have few options about when and where to deliver the message.

The client's perception of the message may also depend on its form. Here, an important question is whether the message should be delivered orally or in writing. On the one hand, oral advice has a higher risk of misperception or misinterpretation than a written message. On the other hand, a written message may never be read and therefore never perceived. It offers the advisor no immediate opportunity to drive home a point and to clarify its meaning through interaction and dialogue with the client.

In many situations, the advisor should deliver the message both in writing and orally. Even here, one may need to decide which comes first. Depending on the nature of the client and the problem, it may be better to offer the oral advice first and to follow up with a written memorandum to drive home the point, or, instead, to present the written memo first to permit reflection by the client and then follow up with a face-to-face meeting to explain and amplify the written message. For example, a doctor who has diagnosed a patient with cancer would probably first inform the patient orally in a private meeting and follow up with a letter specifying the nature of the disease and the appropriate treatment. On the other hand, a management consultant recommending a new marketing strategy to a client might first describe it in a report and then make an oral presentation.

Interpretation

Once clients have perceived the message, they must next interpret it to understand its meaning. *Interpretation* has to take place if the client is to have the benefit of the advisor's message. At a minimum, the patient who hears that he is HIV positive must come to understand that he risks developing AIDS and that he must therefore take precautions in sexual relations to prevent transmitting the infection to others. And the senate candidate who is told "Don't take a position on free trade" must understand those words to mean he should avoid making statements in speeches and interviews that endorse the idea of free exchange of goods and services among nations without regard to domestic consequences.

Every profession has its own special language. It is the language in which professionals are trained, and it becomes part of their everyday work. It also can be a great obstacle to communicating with clients. On the one hand, technical terms give precision to meaning. They allow an advisor to describe a situation precisely and to distinguish one kind of condition from another. Consequently, technical language is essential in making a precise analysis of a problem and finding an appropriate solution. For example, a CPA advising on the worth of a business would consider the difference between book value and market value to be vital and obvious. On the other hand, the fact that an understanding of technical terms requires long study means that clients without special training will not readily understand them. So the technical language of the doctor, lawyer, engineer, or other professionals can become a barrier between them and their clients. Technical language can obstruct the client's interpretation of the message. The challenge for the advisor is to overcome these barriers by communicating in language that the client understands. Meeting this challenge is not always easy.

For many advisors, the use of technical language, with colleagues and clients alike, is part of their identity and status. It is one way for professionals to demonstrate to the world that they are experts and therefore worthy of special respect. As a result, they may feel that communicating in another fashion will diminish their status, so they may be reluctant to talk like laypersons. Equally important, advisors may not have been trained to communicate in any other way. They must therefore learn this skill themselves. Like a good teacher, a skillful advisor can draw on a variety of techniques to make technical concepts clear to untrained persons. Here are a few examples:

First, as was pointed out in chapter 2, know the client. With this knowledge, you will be able to tailor your communication in a way that will help your clients understand your message. For example, if you are advising an experienced business executive on the worth of a business, you can probably assume that he will understand the difference between book and market value. But if you are advising his heir, a professor of art history, you probably need to explain both terms when you use them.

Second, anticipate which particular terms and concepts will cause the most difficulty for clients and therefore prepare in advance everyday equivalents that they will easily understand.

Third, use concrete examples and analogies to help the client understand technical terms. To the extent practical, those examples should be drawn from or related to the client's own experience so that they are readily understandable. For example, a management consultant helping an African agricultural cooperative improve its accounting will communicate more effectively by using examples from a small store or factory rather than from a giant multinational corporation like IBM. Stories are powerful mechanisms for seizing and holding clients' attention. You can often deliver your message effectively by using stories to present your concrete examples.

Fourth, make drawings, sketches, and diagrams to give the client a concrete understanding of technical language. A picture is indeed worth a thousand words. A doctor explaining the impact of a hormone treatment might give the client a clear idea by sketching the effect of the drug on the targeted organ. An appropriate graph in a management consultant's report can capture quickly and dramatically the change in a company's profit situation over a period of several years—far more persuasively than three pages of text.

Fifth, find an interpreter. Advisors who do not have the skill or time to communicate effectively with clients sometimes seek the help of persons who do. For example, engineering consultants may hire former English teachers to write clear reports for clients. Some large hospitals assign a nurse the job of keeping families of patients undergoing major, lengthy surgery informed of what is happening in the operating room. Often an interpreter participates in the advising process without the advisor's direct knowledge. Thus the secretaries of doctors and lawyers often explain what their bosses have said to clients who still have questions after a consultation. In most cases, advisors should recognize the important role that their assistants play as interpreters and help them to do the job effectively.

The truly artful advisor seeks ways to conceptualize, to clarify, and to simplify situations, options, and choices. But that search must begin with the advisor's recognition that the risk of misunderstanding is always present throughout the advising process. At each step of the way, and with each transmission, advisors should ask themselves: How might I be misunderstood?

Feedback

The advising process does not stop with the mere delivery of the message. A major challenge for any advisor is to be sure that the client interprets the message as the advisor intended. How is an advisor to determine what is actually going on in a client's mind? The principal source of this information is *feedback*. For every advisor's statement that is perceived and interpreted by the client, there is a reaction, however slight, by the client to that statement. That reaction is feedback. The look of shock on the patient's face when she learns she has skin cancer is feedback—a clear indication that the patient has perceived and interpreted the message. Nodding agreement by the senate candidate who is told "Don't take a position on free trade" is feedback. Feedback is valuable information to the advisor because it indicates whether and how the client has perceived and interpreted the message. Just as the candidate's nod tells the advisor something, the lack of a nod says something else. Feedback, of course, may be ambiguous. The politician's nod to his consultant can mean many things: "I agree," "I heard you," or "Let's get on to the next subject."

For feedback to be useful, the advisor must perceive and interpret it, just as the client has to perceive and interpret the original message. And should feedback indicate that the client has not fully understood the message, the advisor must then *retransmit* it in another form so that the client may better understand the meaning of the message. For the retransmission to be meaningful, the client must also perceive and interpret it in a way that the advisor intended. Thus the communication process is a continuing chain represented in the diagram on the following page.

MAKE IT CONSTRUCTIVE

The advising process must not only be clear, it must also be constructive. A skillful advisor tries to be constructive throughout the advising process, but two rules are particularly important:

1. Be constructive in understanding the client's problem.
2. Be constructive in recommending solutions.

Many advisors, particularly in the early years of their careers, are fundamentally negative in carrying out the advising process. They tend to stress the severity of the client's situation or they concentrate on recommending against certain courses of action. They may behave in this way out of conviction or for reasons of self-interest. For example, they may think that the more bleak they paint the client's predicament, the more the client will need the advisor and, if the advice works,

PHASES OF ADVISOR-CLIENT COMMUNICATION

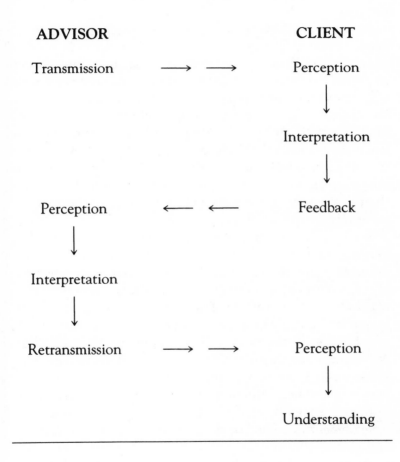

ADVISOR		CLIENT
Transmission	→ →	Perception
		↓
		Interpretation
		↓
Perception	← ←	Feedback
↓		
Interpretation		
↓		
Retransmission	→ →	Perception
		↓
		Understanding

value the advisor's services. Then, too, they may feel it is safer to recommend against, rather than for, certain actions, since they believe that the risk of failure is less when the client does nothing.

A pessimistic advisor is not generally the best advisor. Indeed, consistently negative advice is often an indication of inexperience. While formal education may have taught advisors what won't work, it's experience that teaches them what will. It is important to remember, as chapter 3 indicated, that an advisor's basic purpose is to help clients deal with their problems. Clients are better equipped to assume that task when they believe that help is possible. One of the talents of the effective advisor is to make the client see the positive opportunities in a situation, to see the glass as half full rather than half empty, to view a problem as a chance for improvement rather than a certainty for disaster.

If clients are in some way responsible for or linked to the existing state of affairs, advisors need to be cautious in their negative criticism. In particular, an advisor must make the client understand that criticism of the situation is not criticism of the client. Thus a financial consultant reviewing the chaotic inventory controls of a small office supply company should avoid saying to the owner, "How could you let yourself get into a mess like this?" or "Whoever set this system up didn't know much about accounting." Those gratuitous comments, which contribute nothing to improving the company's situation, will only offend the owner and therefore prevent the development of a good working relationship between advisor and client.

A client can be offended by negative criticism in less obvious ways. In one case, an international agency assigned an

American banker for six months to advise the Central Bank of an African country, a former colony of France, on ways to improve the evaluation of loans made by local commercial banks. During his assignment, the advisor often criticized the country's French-style system of accounting. Once he told the bank's deputy governor, "Only a mindless Francophile could love this system." On another occasion, during a seminar with bank officials, he remarked, "Nobody really understands this system, but then nobody really understands anything the French do, anyway." While the American advisor may have assumed that the country's unhappy colonial experience with France would make the bank's officials receptive to his comments, the deputy governor of the Central Bank, an ardent nationalist, was in fact deeply offended. Having studied at the University of Paris, married a Frenchwoman, and actually lived in France for ten years, he interpreted the American's comments as personal criticism, as an accusation that he was a "mindless Francophile." At the end of the American's contract, when the international agency asked the Central Bank if it wanted to extend the consultancy for an additional six months, the deputy governor politely declined the offer. The advisor would have been far more effective had he limited himself to analyzing the weaknesses and strengths of the existing system without turning his consultancy into an opportunity to evaluate all of French culture—something that was completely outside of his assignment and which he was totally unqualified to undertake.

Being constructive does not mean being overly optimistic or telling your clients only what they want to hear. A good advisor is not a yes-man. What clients seek from an advisor is balanced judgment. While negative advice may prevent clients from making mistakes, it does not offer them definite ways of improving their situation. Early in his career as advisor to presidents, Henry Kissinger learned what most counselors come to know instinctively through experience, that a president is often surrounded by people telling him what he cannot do, but that "it is better to become one of those telling him what he can do or at least offering preferable alternatives."[*]

The importance of offering preferable alternatives cannot be understated. In any situation where an advisor recommends against a certain action, he or she should always offer another option for positive action. For example, a college student, attracted by the theater, approaches his drama professor to obtain advice about dropping out of school to make a career on Broadway. The professor advises against this action because it would mean the student's loss of a university degree that might be valuable later in life. In addition, he feels that the student, while talented, is not mature enough to face the rigors of life in New York City. Rather than simply disapprove of the student's plan to leave the university, the professor also offers to help the student obtain parts in local theater productions in a nearby city while continuing his studies. The professor thus gives the student a constructive alternative.

Another dimension of being constructive is to develop recommendations that the client can easily act upon. The role of the advisor is not to deliver learned opinions on the state of the client or the state of the world but rather to help the client formulate a plan of action to address a problem. In this respect, the advisor must understand the client's capabilities

[*] Walter Isaacson, *Kissinger: A Biography* (New York: Simon & Schuster, 1992), p. 113.

to implement what is recommended. Often, advisors deliver general advice that clients understand but do not know how to translate into action. For example, one foreign economic advisor to an Eastern European country strongly recommended that all unprofitable state industries be sold to foreign investors or local entrepreneurs, but he failed to say what the government should do about the hundreds of thousands of unionized workers in state enterprises who faced the loss of their jobs as a result of this proposed change. In short, the economist's advice was not actionable. Because it was not actionable, the government ignored it. The foreign economist's advice was not constructive because it was incomplete. Either deliberately or ignorantly, he failed to foresee an important negative consequence of his recommendation and to provide advice on how to deal with it.

Delphic advice is another form of unconstructive counsel. Like the oracle of Delphi in ancient Greece, some modern advisors give their clients advice that is either too ambiguous or too obscure to be used. Contemporary Delphic advisors advise clients to sell their stocks "when the market hits its peak" or to bomb the Iraqis until they "feel the pain." Incomplete or Delphic advice allows advisors to escape both the hard choices in giving advice to clients and the harsh consequences of client decisions that are wrong. Neither type of advice helps the client, and much of it can hurt as well. To avoid the pitfalls of Delphi, skilled modern advisors should evaluate each bit of advice they give against the action test: If I were the client, would I be able to take constructive action on the basis of this advice? If the answer to that question is no, then you ought not to give it or at least be prepared to help your client work through it.

As you seek to devise a constructive advising process for your clients, remember these three simple rules:

1. Accentuate the positive.
2. Don't emphasize the negative.
3. Always offer actionable, helpful options.

7
KEEP
YOUR ADVICE
PURE

"And certain it is, that the light a man
receiveth by counsel from another, is
drier and *purer,* than that which
cometh from his own understanding
and judgment; which is ever infused
and drenched, in his affectations and
customs."
—Bacon, "Of Friendship"

PURE ADVICE

IN THE WORDS OF SIR FRANCIS BACON, the advantage of another
person's advice is that it affords a "drier and purer" light for
solving a problem than does the light that clients themselves
can provide. In theory, by virtue of their detachment, advisors are able to give objective, independent counsel that is
unaffected by the client's own biases, fears, and blind spots.
In practice, however, an advisor's light can sometimes also
be impure. Advice can be contaminated by the advisor's own
biases, fears, and self-interest. Effective advisors are alert to
the risks of impurities in the advising process, and they take

steps to guard against them. They know that a fundamental rule of the art of advice is to keep their advice pure.

Advice is a powerful force. Like a miracle drug that cures infections, good advice can reform an organization, strengthen a government, or change a life. But like a drug, advice usually works only when it is pure. The ability of an antibiotic to stop infection depends on its purity. If dust contaminates the manufacturing process, the drug will fail to cure the disease, and it may even kill the patient. Similarly, impurities can also intrude into the advising process. When that happens, impure advice can cause an organization to collapse, a government to fall, and a life to be ruined.

When is advice impure? Just because advice turns out to be wrong does not mean it was impure. The diligent financial advisor who erroneously urged her clients to sell their stocks a week before the stock market soared did not necessarily provide impure advice. The same is true of the doctor who recommends an experimental drug that fails to slow the onset of AIDS. After all, no advisor can be expected to guarantee the future in all cases.

Rather, advisors give impure advice when they fail to fulfill their two fundamental obligations to the client: their duty of *loyalty* and their duty of *care*. What clients expect—whether they are prisoners in a cell, patients in a hospital, or executives in a boardroom—is, first, that their advisors will place clients' interests above their own; and, second, that their advisors will look after those interests carefully. Loyalty and care are what clients expect and what skilled advisors learn to deliver.

Unfortunately, advisors sometimes allow the impurities of self-interest, prejudice, and carelessness to creep into the advising process and prevent clients from getting what they deserve. Let us explore the nature of these impurities and suggest ways that the effective advisor may guard against them.

THE LOYAL ADVISOR

In the modern era, when market forces seem to determine so many issues, the notion of loyalty has a quaint, almost old-fashioned ring. In business and government today, it is self-interest, not loyalty, that seems to be the driving force. Who, after all, serves another out of loyalty? Lawyers serve their clients to earn a fee. Doctors work hard to heal the sick, but few would say that they are loyal to their patients. For international consultants, who often see themselves as hired guns in an age of laptop computers and cellular telephones, loyalty to the client may appear to have gone the way of manual typewriters and carbon paper—a quality that once was useful but has now been replaced by something else.

Yet the fundamental duty of advisors is to advance the interests of the client and not to use their position to further their own interests in any way that the client has not specifically approved and accepted. It is in this sense that an effective advisor is loyal to a client.

Advisors, by virtue of their position, have a relationship of trust and confidence with their clients. Because of that relationship, clients come to depend on their advisors. In that situation, the ordinary rules of the marketplace do not and ought not apply. A client is not just an ordinary buyer, and an advisor is not just one more seller. On the contrary, in law virtually all advisors who have a relationship of trust and confidence with their clients are considered to be *fiduciaries*—"persons who have a duty, created by their undertaking to act primarily for the benefit of another in matters connected with that undertaking."* Derived from the Latin *fiducia* for "trust," fiduciaries must be faithful—loyal to the trust that has been placed in them. So while *caveat emptor*—"let the buyer beware"—may be the traditional rule in the sale of goods (although modern notions of consumer protection have changed that old rule as well), it has never been the guiding principle in relations between advisors and clients.

Both ethical and pragmatic reasons explain the special duty of loyalty that advisors owe their clients. First, clients have traditionally based their relationship with advisors on trust and confidence, with the result that the client is *dependent* on the advisor. To allow the advisor to exploit that dependency for personal benefit would be unethical.

Why has a similar dependency relationship not traditionally existed in the sale of goods? It may be that whereas a buyer has an independent means, at least in theory, to verify the quality and quantity of goods purchased, clients who seek out advisors because of the latter's superior knowledge are unable to verify advice in the same way that they would the quality of a bale of cotton or the quantity of a load of wood. In short, while society may consider buyers and sellers in the market to be equals, advisors and clients, because of differences in knowledge, cannot be considered equals in the same way.

Second, and just as important, whereas markets can function efficiently when operating on the principle of "let the buyer beware," advising relationships cannot. In most instances, if advising is to achieve its goal, which is to help the client, the client must rely at least to some degree on the advisor. The client must confide in and trust the advisor. A client company must open its books to its management

---

* *Black's Law Dictionary*, p. 753.

consultant, and an emotionally disturbed teenager must reveal his thoughts to the psychotherapist. For doctor and patient, lawyer and client, or consultant and company to remain at arm's length from each other throughout the advising process, like buyers and sellers in a market, would greatly reduce the efficacy of advising and limit its usefulness. So for these ethical and practical reasons, advisors and clients have a special relationship, in most cases a *fiduciary* relationship, which means that advisors have a duty of loyalty to their clients.

THE DEMANDS OF LOYALTY

As an advisor, you can fail in your duty of loyalty to your client's interests in many different ways. The initial test of loyalty faced by an advisor usually comes in deciding whether or not to accept someone as a client. At this point, advisors must balance their natural desire to gain a client, earn a fee, or influence another person against their evaluation of whether they really have the ability to help the client with a problem. You are disloyal as an advisor if you accept a client when you know you have neither the knowledge nor experience to help.

Your second duty of loyalty is simply to do for your client what you promised. By becoming an advisor, whether to a national government or to your next-door neighbor, you make commitments to others, commitments that raise expectations, commitments that other persons will rely upon. As a transportation consultant to an Asian government, you agree to make an analysis of competing ports in the region and propose a plan to expand the amount of cargo traffic through that country's own ports. Your next-door neighbor is about to lose her job and you agree to review her résumé and to suggest companies where she might seek work. Your promise in the first case would take the form of a lengthy contract, and in the second in a casual conversation over the backyard fence. In either case, you are disloyal to your client if you fail to do what you promised.

A third type of disloyalty occurs when you use your position as advisor to profit at your clients' expense without their knowledge and consent. For example, a financial consultant who secretly acts as an advisor to both buyer and seller in a company takeover would clearly be violating a duty of loyalty to both clients. Similarly, an advisor who obtained confidential information from one client and then sold it to that client's competitor would certainly be acting disloyally toward the first client. And the false information that Iago, for motives of vengeance, gave to Othello to make him doubt Desdemona's faithfulness was also a case of an advisor giving impure advice to a client.

Disloyalty can also take place if you withhold valuable information from a client. For example, a mineral company hires a consulting engineer to evaluate land on which it has an option to purchase. During the course of his work, the engineer comes to believe that an adjoining tract also has valuable mineral deposits. If instead of telling his client about his beliefs the engineer purchased the adjoining tract for himself, he would be violating his duty of loyalty to his client. The consultant gained that information as part of his assignment from the company, and the company was entitled to receive all of the information gathered in the course of the job. In most cases, the courts could force the engineer to turn the land over to the company.

An advisor's disloyal gain need not come at the expense of the client. An advisor does not have to hurt a client to be disloyal. A management consultant who buys the stock of a client company while working on that client's new marketing campaign would violate the duty of loyalty owed to the client, but in most cases would not injure the company. Yet at least one internationally known consulting firm has made such stock purchases by employees grounds for dismissal.

One may well ask why advisors should not be able to profit from their positions if they do not do so at the expense of the client. After all, while it is clear that the mineral company is hurt when the consulting engineer withholds information about minerals on an adjoining tract of land, how does a management consultant harm a client company by buying a few hundred shares of its stock? Under many laws and ethical codes, the test of disloyalty is not injury to the client but rather unauthorized gain by the advisor. The rule prohibiting such activity rests principally on two reasons. First, clients are entitled to assume that their advisors will devote full attention and efforts to working on their problems and will not be diverted by considerations of personal gain. Second, the prohibition on unauthorized profit seeks to remove all temptations to act against clients' interests on the assumption that the advisors' goals and those of clients will inevitably come into conflict. Thus the management consultant who owns stock in a client's company may later be influenced by that fact in the advice he gives.

There are basically two ways in which disloyal advisors try to take advantage of their advising relationship for their personal profit: (1) by influencing the client to do something in the advisor's interest, or (2) by using the information or position gained from the advising relationship in transactions with other people. The financial consultant who persuades a client to invest in a business in which the advisor owns an

interest is an example of the first and the management consultant who buys stock in a client's competitor an example of the
second.

The conflict between client interests and advisor interests
is actually or potentially present in every advising relationship.
So the risk if not the reality of disloyalty always exists. A
management consultant to a corporation may believe that his
advice is driven only by what is best for that company. But
consciously or unconsciously, the prospect of future contracts
with that company may influence his advice—for example,
how he now evaluates the performance of company officers
who will be in a position to award those future contracts. A
government lawyer may believe she is offering objective advice
on tax policy to the U.S. Treasury Department; but, then
again, that advice may be affected by her plans to enter private
law practice to represent companies covered by the new tax
law. A young faculty member may schedule lengthy advising
sessions with a female student in order to provide extensive
comments on her thesis, but the professor's physical attraction
to the student may influence his choice of the time and place
of the meetings. An investment banking house that both
advises companies on their initial public offerings of stock
and then sells those shares to the public may indeed provide
objective advice on the appropriate offering price for the stock,
but that advice may also be shaped by its desire to give a
good deal to its large customers who buy those shares. The
management consultant, lawyer, professor, and investment
banking house who give advice in order to advance their
individual interests violate their duty of loyalty to the client,
to the company, to the Treasury Department, to the student,
and to the corporation going public.

THE FORCES OF DISLOYALTY

External forces may influence an advisor to provide counsel that does not advance clients' real interests. One such force may be the clients themselves. A patient, for example, may demand that a doctor prescribe a sedative that the patient has become dependent upon even though the doctor knows it would be better to find ways to eliminate the dependency. A company president may try to influence the final report of a management consultant in a way that will justify the president's decisions. A high school student may seek to persuade a guidance counselor to recommend a certain college because of its social activities rather than its academic program. In these cases, the advisor will often be torn between the need to do what is in the client's best interests and the desire to please—and perhaps even retain—the client.

A second powerful external force leading an advisor to deviate from strict loyalty may come from other clients. For example, one client company may want you to share information that you learned while working for another client company. Or hearing of your work as a consultant to the Environmental Protection Agency on the preparation of new regulations for the storage of toxic wastes, a chemical company asks you to counsel it about ways to comply with the regulations at less cost or avoid them altogether. Certainly if you gave the EPA advice in a way that created technical loopholes for the chemical companies you planned to counsel later, your advice would be tainted and you would violate your ethical and legal responsibilities to the agency. If your advice was not influenced by your future plans, then it would have been pure at the time, but your work for the chemical company may still be flawed if you used confidential information that you gained at the EPA.

By virtue of the advising relationship, your client is entitled to expect that you are not subjected to influences, pressures, and temptations that may cause you to give impure advice. For example, your brother-in-law is the president of a shoe company. A competing shoe company, unaware of your family relationship, wants to hire you to advise them on a new marketing campaign. Even though you are absolutely convinced of your ability to prepare a dynamic campaign and are certain that you will not be influenced by your brother-in-law (whom you don't like anyway), you fail in your duty of loyalty to your client if you do not disclose your potential conflict of interest. The shoe company should receive all the necessary facts about your potentially conflicting relationships and then have the opportunity to make its own decision as to whether or not it wants to hire you for the new campaign. You have no right to make that decision for them. Disclosure of potential conflicts of interest is the most effective way of handling these problems. Just as strong sunlight can purify, so too can disclosure purify a potential conflict of interest. As a general rule, an advisor should reveal to the client those facts that the client would consider significant in deciding whether to use the advisor or the advice given.

Similarly, the ability of an advisor to profit from an advising relationship may also depend on the knowledge and agreement of the client. For example, the consulting engineer who discovers mineral deposits on land adjoining the client's could ethically and legally purchase them if he told the client of his findings and obtained approval to make the purchase. And an investment bank might legally provide advice to both buyer and seller in the negotiation of a sale of a company if both knew and agreed to the bank's participation.

Individual laws and ethical codes applicable to a particular profession may define the nature of an advisor's duty of loyalty differently. Activity that is considered an illegal conflict of interest in one occupation may be permitted in another. Some advisors, like lawyers, are highly regulated in their relationship with their clients. Others, like financial consultants, are not. Any advisor should, of course, fully understand the codified legal and ethical obligations owed to clients. And certainly all advisors should seek to meet those obligations out of a respect for the law, professional codes, and their own sense of morality. But regardless of the precise scope of those obligations, as defined in law, codes, and ethics, all advisors, regardless of occupation, should recognize that they have a general duty of loyalty to their clients and that the fulfillment of that duty is essential to their effectiveness as advisors. Despite the possession of advanced university degrees and many years of experience, a disloyal advisor is, in the end, an incompetent advisor.

THE CAREFUL ADVISOR

Care is an advisor's second basic duty to the client. The duty of care is a complex notion that implies that advisors will devote serious attention, diligence, and their full skills to the task of advising. It does not mean that an advisor must guarantee the results of the advice given, but neither does it mean *caveat emptor*, let the *client* beware. Rather, it means let the advisor take care. The advisor should take care to perform the advising task carefully. Here, the impurity that advisors must guard against is that of carelessness.

Like disloyalty, carelessness can take many forms. Carelessness can mean, first of all, accepting an advising assignment without being reasonably sure that you have the knowledge or skill to help the client. Consequently, a minister without psychological training who tries to advise a suicidal teenager may be violating a duty of care. When you are not sure that you have adequate training, you should refer the potential client to someone who does. The minister, then, should send the suicidal parishioner to a psychiatrist, rather than try to deal with the problem directly.

A second major form of carelessness occurs when the advisor does not devote the time and attention required to help the client. A faculty advisor who merely signs a student's course selection form for the semester without reading or discussing it with the student fails in his or her duty of care to the student. A consulting engineer who writes a report without visiting the construction site is also giving advice that is impure, to say the least. A doctor who dismisses as "just a cold sore," without close examination or tests, a persistent lesion on a patient's lip that later turns out to be cancerous also fails in her duty of care to the patient.

Failures in your duty of care can happen in other, less blatant ways. For example, unconscious biases and prejudices can erroneously influence the kind of advice you give to a client. Care means that you see your client as an individual, not as a stereotype. The failure to know your clients, as chapter 2 discusses, instead treating them as types, leads to impure advice. So the high school guidance counselor who consistently steers white children from the suburbs toward Ivy League colleges and African-American students from the inner city toward technical schools is failing to see clients as individuals. Similarly, a study found that doctors were ten times more likely to send men with signs of heart trouble for angiograms than they were women, and three times more likely to attribute chest pains in women to psychiatric reasons. The risk of stereotyping clients exists in all professions. And many professionals rely on them to save the time, energy, and resources needed to understand each client as an individual. The use of stereotypes is, among other things, a failure of care that the advisor owes to the client.

THE COSTS OF IMPURE ADVICE

The client is not the only one to bear the costs of impure advice. The advisor also has to bear the consequences. Generally, these consequences are of three types: an obligation to compensate an injured client, a negative impact on the advisor's reputation, or sanctions imposed by the state or a professional organization that limit or prohibit the advisor's activities in the future. Thus, through the courts, a financial advisor who has made a profit on investments at a widow's expense will have to pay the profits to the client, and a consulting engineer who carelessly approved the construction of a building that later collapsed will be liable to compensate the client for the loss caused by the negligent consulting report. In addition, both the engineer and the financial consultant may be prevented temporarily or permanently from practicing their professions in the future. And if their actions are severe enough, they may even face criminal penalties.

KEEPING YOUR ADVICE PURE

Since all advisors run the risk of giving impure advice, how should they protect themselves against this possibility? What mechanisms should they install to keep their advice pure? Here are a few simple suggestions that may help you fulfill your duties of loyalty and care to your clients.

1. Know your own weaknesses. To develop defenses against failing in your duties as an advisor, you first need to know your own weaknesses and failings. You need to know yourself. A place to begin is to recognize that you, like all other advisors, are potentially susceptible to conflicts of interest, carelessness, and bias. The most dangerous attitude of all for you as an advisor is to believe that these all too human failings are beneath you. Do not assume that you are more ethical than everybody else.

Psychiatrists are required to undergo psychoanalysis not only to understand the process that their clients will experience but also to better know themselves. Few other advising professions require their members to engage in such intensive self-examination. Indeed, some professions like medicine and law seem to do just the opposite. Their professional schools inculcate in students a sense of superiority—even invincibility—rather than a deeper understanding of themselves as human beings with specific strengths and weaknesses. So law students are constantly told to "think like a lawyer," as if it were a superhuman form of reasoning, and medical students gain the idea that their advanced medical knowledge somehow makes them invincible.

As a piece of advice, "Know your own weaknesses" has a definite Delphic ring. It sounds much like a vague and ambiguous pronouncement from the oracle. How specifically is an advisor to make that bit of advice actionable?

Your ability to understand your own weaknesses will depend greatly on your own powers of introspection and self-examination. But you can do a few things to help things along.

First, recognize the limits of your own knowledge and expertise. Determine the areas that your training and experience have not prepared you to enter. Second, keep a journal or a record of your own advising experiences. Actually having to think about and record what you said and did will give you strong indications of what you did right and what you did wrong. Third, using your journal, or just your memory, review your past instances of advising to find consistent patterns of how you behaved in your role as advisor. Do you have a tendency to take on too many commitments to clients in too short a time? Do you delay in completing certain types of assignments? Do you get angry with certain types of clients? Fourth, by contact with your colleagues or through attendance at professional seminars, identify models of good advising practice. Try to determine why those persons are good advisors, and then compare your own ways of advising to theirs.

2. Identify your client's interests and your own interests in each advising relationship. In each advising relationship, you need to determine your client's interests if you are going to help. But you also need to be clear on your own interests. You have a definite interest in any advising relationship. You are never a totally altruistic advisor. You certainly have your fee to collect, or at least your reputation to protect. But you may have other interests as well. For example, your son asks for advice on a career. Will you be guided only by parental love and altruism? Or will you also be influenced by your own desire for increased financial security in your old age or the impact on your family reputation of his choosing a job whose status does not meet your own aspirations? It may be helpful to write down your client's interests and your own interests in separate columns and then to compare them for similarities and conflicts. If conflicts exist, be sure to discuss them fully with the client before the two of you negotiate your role.

3. Create and follow procedures. Every advising profession has established procedures for carrying out particular advising tasks. Doctors interview and examine patients in accordance with a defined series of steps. Consulting economists apply definite methodologies in making their forecasts. Investment advisors fill out forms to report their own investments. These procedures are not just mindless bureaucracy. They are designed to implement the advisor's duties of care and loyalty. As an advisor, you should apply those procedures to your work. If you are a consultant in a field in which there are no established procedures, you should create them with the goal of ensuring your loyalty to and care for your clients. One of the most basic, helpful procedures for any professional advisor is to keep an accurate record of every advising case.

4. Try not to work alone. Like a client, an advisor can always benefit from the drier and purer light of another person's counsel. Such counsel can help advisors keep their own advice pure. The views of another person can allow advisors to see their weaknesses, their conflicts of interest, and their failures to fulfill their duties of loyalty and care. The importance of another view would argue for advisors to work in teams. Often, however, this is not possible. Nonetheless, every advisor should have someone to whom he or she can turn for advice and counsel on difficult cases. For a lawyer, this may be an experienced attorney in the next office. For a doctor, it may be a senior colleague down the hall.

The truly dangerous advisor is the one who works like an oracle—alone and accountable to no one.

8

AGREE ON
THE END
AT THE BEGINNING

"A bad beginning makes a bad ending."
—Euripides, *Aeolus*

GREAT ARTISTS BEGIN A WORK OF ART with a vision of the end. Michelangelo saw in a discarded block of marble the magnificence of *David*, and Mozart heard in the quiet of his rooms the overpowering strains of the *Requiem*. Advisors, too, must undertake their task with a vision of the end—with a clear perception of their goals in advising a particular client.

A vision of the end has two basic functions: It guides both artists and advisors in their work, and it allows both artist and advisor to know when they have attained their goals. In short, a vision helps you to know when to stop. Just as Michelangelo knew that at some point he would complete his statue and need to lay down his hammer and chisel, artistic advisors know that at some point in the advisory relationship their clients will no longer need them. In undertaking any work of art, the artist must know when to stop. The failure to stop at the right moment can be the difference between a perfect and flawed performance. Like Michelangelo who knew exactly at what point he should stop chipping at *David*, the skilled advisor must also recognize at what point advice is no longer needed or desirable. Experienced advisors also know that more advice than is necessary, no matter how well intended, may actually hurt the client, just as adding a few extra bars of music to the *Requiem* would have diminished its effect.

THE EXCESSES OF ADVICE

For the advisor, like the artist, knowing precisely when to stop is not always easy. Some stop too soon and therefore fail to help clients fully with their problems. Others have a tendency to overadvise, to continue giving counsel even when it is no longer necessary. Too much advising can be harmful to your client. The specific nature of that harm may vary from client to client but basically there are three general types:

Unnecessary Dependency

By the very nature of the advising relationship, the client is dependent on the advisor. In most—if not all—cases, the purpose of that relationship is to help solve clients' problems and therefore end that dependency. The aim of a psychotherapist counseling troubled teenagers is to enable them to deal with their problems by themselves, to reach the point where they will no longer need the psychotherapist. The task of a business consultant advising a failing company is to resolve its financial crisis so that the consultant's services will no longer be necessary—at least with respect to that particular problem. Although clients begin by being dependent on their advisors, their ultimate goal in the relationship is to attain the status of independence. The psychotherapist or business consultant who continues to advise a client on a specific problem beyond what is necessary to solve that problem is maintaining the client in a state of unnecessary dependency and is therefore failing in the advisor's fundamental duty—to help the client.

Certainly many advisory relationships are long-term or even semipermanent. You may have the same physician all your life, a family lawyer whom you regularly call for advice, and a business consultant who periodically reviews your company's procedures. The length of the relationship itself does not cause unnecessary dependency. Rather, it is the way the advisor manages that relationship that leads to overadvising.

Unnecessary Costs

Too much advising usually entails unnecessary costs, and it is almost always the client who has to pay them. The political consultant who wants to take one more public opinion poll before advising the political candidate on a campaign strategy may indeed want further data but she may also be incurring additional expense that will tell the campaign organization nothing more than it knows already. A doctor may want to put a patient with back pains through one more set of tests to reconfirm the diagnosis already made, but those extra tests will increase the costs of advice by several thousand dollars. Overadvising can take many forms—additional surveys, extra assistants, further studies, more counseling sessions—all of which amount to added costs for the client. Here, the principle of proportionality applies: The cost of the advice should bear a reasonable relationship to its value to the client.

Determining proportionality in a specific case is never easy. One can offer no firm rules that apply to all advisors. One can only urge every advisor to consider the issue of proportionality of costs throughout the advising relationship. Too often advisors assume that all expenses incurred in giving their advice are automatically worth the cost.

Opportunity Costs

Not stopping at the right time can also mean lost opportunities for your client. A foreign policy advisor who insists on lengthy studies before giving an opinion to a president facing a crisis may cause the president to miss a chance to take an action at the right moment to solve the crisis. A psychotherapist who continues treatment of a healthy patient may cause that client to miss opportunities for a job, a new group of friends, an independent life. A parent who insists on continuing to review and revise a daughter's résumé before allowing it to be sent to prospective employers may be causing her to miss the peak of the hiring season. Thus an advisor who does not know when to stop can cause a client to pay both real costs and opportunity costs.

IMPEDIMENTS TO STOPPING AT THE RIGHT TIME

Advisors are uncertain about when to stop advising because several factors can impair their vision. First, of course, is uncertainty over whether the client's problem has actually been solved. Determining whether a patient has regained health or whether a company has actually achieved stable profitability is not always clear, and reasonable advisors may differ in their interpretation of the client's situation. Second, the advisor and client may have different understandings about the goals of the advisory relationship. For example, an executive may have sought a lawyer's help on a specific tax problem in connection with a business transaction, but the lawyer may have assumed that she was also to provide general legal advice for the whole transaction. Third, of course, advisors almost always have a definite self-interest in preserving the advisory relationship as long as possible—often beyond the point when it is no longer needed. That self-interest can take the form of additional consulting fees or merely the ego satisfaction that advisors gain from knowing that another person relies on them. This self-interest can affect the advisor's judgment about the proper moment to stop advising the client. In most cases, it may mean that the advisor will seek to continue advising when advice is no longer needed. How, then, can an advisor know when to stop?

KNOWING WHEN TO STOP

Determining the right time to stop advising is always a matter of judgment. It is not subject to fixed rules. Nevertheless, a basic principle of the art of advice is, *The client and the advisor should plan for the end of the relationship at its beginning.* Like an artist, an advisor must indeed have a vision of the end, but it must be the shared vision of both advisor and client. Often the conflicts and uncertainties that arise between client and advisor over termination of the advisory relationship come about because they do not have a common vision of the end, a clear mutual understanding of the goal they are trying to reach. Consequently, they will want to discuss when to stop in connection with agreeing on the advisor's role, as chapter 4 recommends. As an advisor, your discussions with your client on the end of the relationship will want to deal with two basic questions: the reasons for ending the relationship, and the way it will happen.

On the other hand, no amount of planning and discussion can foresee all possible contingencies that might cause either the client or the advisor to want to end the relationship. Regardless of your plans, you may face the question of termination in the course of the advising process. Here, too, you will need to address the reasons for and the ways of ending the relationship.

REASONS FOR STOPPING

1. Your client has reached the goal. A fundamental reason for ending the advising process is that your client has reached the goal that you both had agreed upon. Here, of course, it is important that both advisor and client agree on a clear goal and then both together recognize when they have attained it.

It sometimes happens that although advisor and client agreed on a goal at the outset, they later disagree on whether it has been reached. For example, a company hires a consultant to advise them on a new communications system. The company believes the relationship will end when it has chosen the system, but the consultant believes the goal will be attained only when the new system is installed and working.

Or a patient seeks a doctor's help for a weight loss program. After losing twenty-five pounds, the patient feels that his weight problem is solved, but the doctor disagrees. Similarly, a Latin American country with rapidly depreciating currency seeks the advice of an international monetary expert to develop policies that will stabilize the situation. After a year, the currency stops its slide, so the government believes it has achieved its goal and no longer needs external advice. The monetary expert, however, thinks the stabilization is only temporary.

Advisor and client at the outset of their relationship need to define what each means by success. To do that, they first must be sure that they have a shared understanding of the words they use. For example, do both computer advisor and client company understand the difference between "selecting" a computer system and "installing" it in the same way? Second, to the extent possible, advisor and client should establish specific, identifiable goalposts—preferably, quantitative—that will tell them whether they have actually reached their goal. Thus a weight loss goal for a patient might be reaching 150 pounds and staying at that weight for six consecutive months, and a monetary stabilization objective might be preserving the value of the peso in the range between 100 and 120 to the U.S. dollar for a period of a year.

2. You are in over your head. You work in the accounting department of a large company but are not a CPA. Your next-door neighbor asks you to help him fill out his tax return and you readily agree. After all, you have done your own taxes all your life and have helped your co-workers fill out their returns many times. Halfway through the process, you discover that your neighbor has a "working interest" (whatever that means) in an oil well in Texas, which paid him significant income during the year and also gave him large deductions for "intangible drilling costs" and "depletion," both of which you know nothing about. Indeed, you have never even read the special tax form that you have to fill out for oil income.

You have encountered a common problem for advisors: You agree to work on what looks like an easy problem at the start but later discover it is more complex than you realized. You are in over your head. Getting in over your head is a risk that every advisor faces in virtually every field of endeavor. A neurologist discovers that a patient with severe headaches has deep psychological problems. A CPA finds that her client has been defrauding the IRS for years and is in danger of criminal prosecution. Both the neurologist and the CPA in these cases face the risk of getting in over their heads unless they take specific action. The patient with bad headaches needs a psychiatrist and the tax cheat needs a criminal lawyer.

When you realize you are in over your head, your only course of action is to explain the situation frankly to your clients and try to refer them to someone who has the knowledge and skill to help them. This situation is never easy for advisors. No one likes to admit ignorance. Your client may have already come to rely on you. You will lose a fee and you may lose the respect of your client. The alternative is to try to muddle through, to attempt to advise in an area that you know nothing or little about. If you do try to muddle through, not only will you fail to help your client but your client may sue you later for damage that you caused. State regulatory agencies or your own professional organization may also punish you because the codes of ethics of almost every profession warn practitioners against offering advice beyond the scope of their training and abilities.

One way to reduce the negative consequence of the unexpected is to plan for your own limitations at the beginning, to make your client aware of the limits of your ability to help, of what you can and cannot do. So you might tell your friend that while you will be glad to help with his tax returns for earned income and capital gains, you really are not an expert on other types of taxation. Once engaged in an advising process, advisors often feel trapped and obliged to push on in cases where they failed to specify the precise extent of their expertise or have allowed their clients to believe that it was greater than it actually was.

3. You don't like your client's behavior. Advising is a relationship, usually a close one, between you and your client. Indeed, as chapter 5 suggests, you and your client are engaged in a duet. You are not giving a solo performance. But what if you don't like the way your client is playing? Suppose you don't like your client's behavior. The varieties of unpleasant client behavior are infinite. Your client does not follow your advice. Your client is hostile to you or abusive to your staff. Your client is always giving you an argument. Your client persists in dangerous or illegal activities, like taking drugs, embezzling from her employer, cheating on his tax returns. Your client is always calling you at home in the late evening about matters that could easily wait until the next morning. Your client will not pay your fees. When are you justified in ending the advising relationship?

Here, too, proper planning at the beginning of the relationship may help you avoid having to face difficult decisions about ending it. You should agree on what clients can expect of you and what you expect of them. If you make clear at the beginning, when you negotiate your role, the factors that may lead you to end the relationship, clients will know first, whether they want to work with you under those conditions, and second, the specific ground rules of the relationship. It is hoped they will behave accordingly.

Dropping a client before resolving the problem can have serious consequences. A political consultant who quits an election campaign because the candidate won't follow advice may effectively kill any chance that the candidate has to win the election. Abandoning a patient who refuses to take prescribed medicine may result in a worsened condition or even death. Dropping a client company in the midst of merger negotiations because the CEO is abrasive under pressure may give you personal satisfaction, but it may also cause the company financial loss. The reason it is so difficult to end the relationship in these situations is that the client has come to depend on you. That dependency did not just happen. In most cases, you fostered and encouraged it by your assurances of help, competence, reliability, care and loyalty. Having helped to create that dependency, you have an ethical and in many cases legal obligation not to withdraw from the relationship in a way that will injure the client. In most cases, you will need to take three steps to withdraw legally and ethically as an advisor:

1. Warn your client about the objectionable behavior and indicate that continuing that behavior may force you to abandon the case.
2. Once you have decided to end the relationship, you should give your client ample notice of the fact so that he or she may obtain the services of another advisor.
3. In many situations, you may also have an obligation to help your client find that other advisor.

4. Your own situation changes. Sometimes your decision to stop is motivated not by your client's behavior but by your own situation. You are ill. You want to retire. You are busy with other matters. You are bored. Here, the advisor's ethical and legal obligations to the client will determine how and under what conditions the advisor may end the relationship. As a general rule, advisory relationships, particularly professional advisory relationships, do not stop simply because the advisor wants them to. Just as a husband and wife must take certain legal steps to divorce, the law or professional codes define what steps must be taken to end the advising relationship. Normally, an advisor has the obligation to give the client ample notice of the impending end of the relationship and then to assist, in varying degrees, the client to find another advisor.

5. The client wants out. While the advisor must ordinarily take special steps to end the relationship, the client is usually free to end it for any reason whatsoever, subject to any financial commitments to the advisor or the provisions of any contract between them. The client is freer to end the relationship than the advisor is because it is the client who is dependent on the advisor, not the reverse.

Experienced advisors are aware of the various ways that the advising relationship may end and they plan for these eventualities at the beginning of the relationship. To paraphrase Euripides, a good beginning is necessary for a good ending.

9

APPRECIATING THE ART OF ADVICE

"I don't know much about
art, but I know what I like."
—Anonymous

NO MATTER HOW MUCH TIME WE SPEND as advisors in our professional lives, we are also clients more often than we are aware. Every day we receive and try to evaluate vast amounts of advice on numerous subjects that we know very little about. Whether we are financial consultants or lawyers, psychiatrists or career counselors, we invariably find ourselves dependent on other advisors, like auto mechanics and plumbers, physicians and interior decorators, in order to function in our everyday lives.

If advice is an art, we are all both artists and art critics. Our ability to appreciate and evaluate the advice we receive is limited by the fact that we often know little about the subject matter. Our advisors usually have much more knowledge than we do about the subject of our problem. That is precisely why we seek their help, and that imbalance of knowledge creates a client's fundamental problem: How can I evaluate an advisor on a subject that I know very little about?

While we may not know about high finance or structural engineering, we can evaluate our financial advisors and engineering consultants by determining *how* effectively they apply the seven principles of the art of advice in their advising relationships with us. While we may not be able to assess their expertise in finance or engineering, we need to remember that expert knowledge alone does not make an effective advisor. Rather, the key question is how effectively the advisor applies that knowledge to resolving our particular problems.

Whether you are a deputy governor of Central Bank dealing with an international consulting firm or a high school student talking to a career counselor, you may begin to evaluate your advisors simply by seeing how well they follow the seven principles of the art of advice discussed in this book:

1. Know your client.
2. Help, or at least do no harm.
3. Agree on your role.
4. Never give a solo performance.
5. Make the process clear and constructive.
6. Keep your advice pure.
7. Agree on the end at the beginning.

For you, as a client, those seven principles translate into seven basic questions that you should ask as you work with your advisor to solve your problems.

1. How well does my advisor know me? An advisor who does not know you really cannot help you. Has your doctor, lawyer, or accountant, as any advisor should, taken the time to learn about your background, your present situation, and your objectives? Has your advisor asked you the three traveler questions: Where have you been? Where are you now? Where do you want to go? Are you a distinct individual to your advisor? Or does the advisor see you as just one more item on a conveyor belt passing in front of him or her?

2. To what extent is my advisor committed to helping me and protecting me from harm? An advising relationship is a power relationship. Your advisor has power basically because you gave it to the advisor. Is your advisor committed to using that power to help you, and does the advisor fully realize that he or she also has the power to hurt you as well?

3. Have I agreed to the role my advisor will play in helping me? You have the right to negotiate the specific role that the advisor will have. Do not allow your advisor to assume or impose a role that you have not agreed to.

4. Is my advisor giving a solo performance? One of the essential points of this book is that advising is a relationship between advisor and client, a relationship in which both people work at solving the client's problem. Do not allow your advisor to work alone. The decision on what to do with the advice you receive is always yours, never your advisor's.

5. Has my advisor made the advising process clear to me, and is my advisor dealing with my problem in a constructive way? The advisor's task is to communicate with you clearly so that you understand *what* he or she is suggesting and *how* that suggestion was arrived at. If you do not understand either of these things, the fault is your advisor's, not yours.

6. Is my advisor's advice free of the impurities of disloyalty and carelessness? Recognize that your advisor may have interests in the advising relationship beyond merely helping you. Try to look at the relationship from your advisor's point of view, and you may begin to understand those interests. Also, carefully evaluate whether your advisor is giving you the time and attention you deserve. Lack of sufficient time and attention is a sure sign of an advisor's lack of care.

7. Has my advisor given me an idea of how the advising relationship will end? The effective advisor communicates to the client the various ways in which the relationship may end. If your advisor neglects to talk about this subject at the beginning, you should raise it on your own.

IN THE STUDIO, NOT THE GALLERY

As you evaluate your advisor, remember that with the right questions you can influence the way your advisor practices his or her art. As a client, you are like a visitor to an artist's studio while the work is being done: You have the opportunity to influence the final product. You are not like the critic who views the completed work in an art gallery. Through the use of the questions and principles discussed in this book, you can be an active client. In this age of advice, with a proliferation of advisors of all types, only an active client is a well-served client.

INDEX

and endings, 136-37
and evaluation of advisors,
147-49
and experience of advisors,
26-28, 35-36, 44
and functions of advisors,
12-15
and judgmental attitudes, 45
and knowing the advisor,
42, 90
and listening, 42-43, 44, 86
and non-verbal
communication, 44-45
and the power of advisors,
16, 17, 18, 43, 54-56,
148
and predicting the future,
58-63
and pure advice, 131
and reliance of clients on
advisors, 16-17, 54-56
and reluctant clients, 89-91
and roles of advisors, 148
and trust, 12, 16-17, 25, 42,
74-75, 83, 122
as a two-way relationship,
12-18
working on the, 82-85
See also Helping/harming;
Roles of advisors
Advisors
advisors to, 134
barriers created by, 25-30

basic task of, 8
benefits/costs of being, 14-18
bias of, 120-21, 131-33
clients as influences on, 149
education of, 101-2
egos of, 28-29, 109
evaluation of, 146-49
finding other, 144
functions/purposes of, 5-6,
12-15, 49, 114
and knowing own
weaknesses, 131-33
limitations of, 141-42
motivations of, 15-16
reasons for choosing, 17-18
self-interest of, 119, 120-21,
138-39
as yes-men, 115-16
Advocacy, 55-57. *See also* Bias
Alternatives. *See* Options
Analogical forecasting, 61-62
Attendants, advisors as, 9-10
Authoritative advisors, 44

Bad news, 50-53
Bank of Credit and Commerce
International, 18
Barriers
and advisor-client
relationships, 25-37, 45
breaking down, 32-37
created by advisors, 25-30
created by clients, 30-31

ABOUT THE AUTHOR

JESWALD W. SALACUSE is dean and Henry J. Braker Professor of Commercial Law at The Fletcher School of Law and Diplomacy, Tufts University. Educated at the Harvard Law School, Hamilton College, and the University of Paris, he has practiced law with a Wall Street firm, taught law in Nigeria, directed a research institute in Zaire, served in Lebanon as the Ford Foundation's advisor on law and development for the Middle East, and established and directed the Ford Foundation program in the Sudan. He was also dean of the School of Law of Southern Methodist University for six years. A member of the Council on Foreign Relations and the American Law Institute, Salacuse lectures widely and advises governments, businesses, universities, foundations, and international organizations in various parts of the world. He lives in Concord, Massachusetts.